HAS KEELE FAILED?

Has Keele Failed?

REFORM IN THE CHURCH OF ENGLAND

Edited by Charles Yeats

Hodder & Stoughton

LONDON SYDNEY AUCKLAND

British Library Cataloguing in Publication Data
A record for this book is available from the British Library

ISBN 0 340 64187 8

Typeset by Phoenix Typesetting, Ilkley, West Yorkshire

Printed and bound in Great Britain by
Cox & Wyman, Reading, Berks.

Hodder and Stoughton Ltd
A Division of Hodder Headline PLC
338 Euston Road
London NW1 3BH

Contents

The mood of the Congress was one of penitence for past failures and of serious resolve for the future. This has meant for many of us not a change of fundamental position, but of stance and even of direction. The *Statement* must not be taken, therefore, as our last and unalterable word. It is more a beginning than an end. As the situation develops, the dialogue increases and the issues clarify, we are sure that we will learn more, and we rather think that we have more to say.

John Stott
from the Introduction to
The Keele Statement, 1967

Foreword

I attended Keele as one of the student delegates. I was in my final year of training at Cranmer Hall, Durham. Michael Saward's essay brought back to me some of the atmosphere of the Congress. It was raw, rough at the edges but with a deep sense of something prophetic and forward looking happening among us. A movement was changing and coming alive in a different way. Most especially a generation of people committed themselves to take their membership of the Church of England seriously and play their part in shaping it for the future.

I was a member of the Church and World section. Was it not in this part of the Conference that we experienced the greatest chaos and the most interesting life? It is fascinating that these essays have not picked up how important this side of the work was. I remember how our section kept the whole final plenary session waiting whilst we argued the final text of our submission! Yet out of this came a generation of people, with some sense of support from the movement, entering into public and political life. From this arose the modern Anglican evangelical movement for social justice. From it has grown a deepening and increasingly skilled contribution to moral theology and social ethics.

Present at Keele were the historic elements of the evangelical movement. Let no one think it has ever been a uniform movement! There were the Puritans and Anabaptists who sat uncomfortably in a comprehensive church. There were the pietists who thought the Church of England the best boat to fish from. There were the young charismatics seeking renewal and revival. There were the radicals who wanted to embrace most things modern. In the midst were a group of leaders, young and old, lay and ordained, who held this disparate and sometimes disorderly movement together – in the best tradition of Cranmer, Hooker, Baxter and Simeon.

I have always thought that the evangelical movement in the Church of England is a bit like the Labour Party. At its best it is exciting, forward looking and rooted in crucial historic values. At its worst it yields to the temptations of all visionary movements to fall apart in squabbling over matters which, in the cold light of day, are not quite as significant as they were thought to be in the heat of the moment.

One of the results of Keele is books of essays of this quality. No doubt readers will react to them in different ways. They are, however, all scholarly, provocative in the best sense, committed to mission in this secular age and concerned for the future of the Church. The debate between David Holloway and Peter Baron picks up the gauntlet thrown down by Robert Runcie at Caistor when he challenged evangelicals to sort out their ecclesiology. Three lay contributions remind us of the crucial significance of lay experience to evangelicalism. An example of this is Ruth Etchells' time as principal of one of the major theological colleges of this tradition. Will the bishops, for example, respond imaginatively to David Day's challenge on lay Presidency? Will the evangelical movement pick up Margaret Masson's crucial questioning of the patriarchal feel of the Church and of evangelicalism in particular? She stands in a long tradition of women in the evangelical movement who have contributed to Christian perspectives in the feminist movement.

Again, these essays demonstrate another strength of the post-Keele movement and that is its sense of the local. This is to be found not only in Michael Wilcock and David Holloway's essays on the parochial foundation of the Church but in the simple fact that a group of people in the north-east have produced a set of major essays. The north-east has long been a centre for Anglican theological work. So how good that the essays include a contribution from the Dean of Durham giving a sense of the comprehensiveness of the Church. His essay on Cathedrals is timely and delightful.

What of the future? We are called to serve the whole Church for the sake of the Gospel and the spiritual health of our people. It will be an act of profound spiritual disobedience if we retreat from this Divine vocation into party-minded squabbling, endless street fighting over trivia and a return to the ghettoes. That would be to deepen the spiritual darkness of this nation and contribute to the further weakening of the Church of God. The real driving power behind the reform of the Church is theological in nature. It is those who have the courage to think and talk of God, to wrestle with the revealed nature of the truth in the context of mission who will, under the Spirit of God, shape the future. Keele had many weaknesses. It did, however, represent the commitment of a generation of evangelical people to the task. That must be continued in our own time.

John Gladwin
Bishop of Guildford
1995

Editor's Introduction

The National Evangelical Congress at Keele in 1967 is widely recognised as having marked the turning point in Anglican evangelicalism in the twentieth century. Before Keele, Anglican evangelicals lived in a kind of Christian ghetto; they concentrated on the parish church and shunned involvement in national and diocesan church structures. After Keele, having repented of their sectarian attitudes, many have moved out into an impressive engagement with the wider Church and the world. In this connection, it is worth quoting the elder statesman of the evangelical movement, John Stott:

> The evangelical party had been guilty of a double withdrawal, withdrawal from the visible Church into the parish, and from the secular world into our own pietistic circles. I think we repented at Keele of both these withdrawals, and the decision to take our place in the Church and in the world was a very significant decision. It has led more than anything else to what has happened since, especially to our most gifted evangelicals getting into synodical government and so on.[1]

But not all evangelicals agree that Keele was or has since been a success. A growing number of disaffected conservative evangelicals, united under the umbrella movement REFORM, even claim that Keele has failed. And so disillusioned are they with what has happened since Keele that they have drawn up plans either to withdraw from the Church of England or to defy diocesan authority by creating a church within a church if their demands are not met. In the meantime, as a form of protest, some parish clergy are exploiting the present weakness in the Church's finances by refusing to pay their parish's full share of the diocesan budget.

The Reverend David Holloway, a founder member of RE-FORM who openly encourages quota-capping, is a good example of one of Keele's evangelical critics. He now claims that Keele has failed. And, reflecting a widespread feeling among conservative evangelicals, he lays the blame at the feet of evangelical bishops, whom he accuses either of having gone 'native', or of allowing their impact as evangelicals to be effectively neutralised by the comprehensiveness of the Church of England.

In support of his accusations, David Holloway specifically mentions the evangelical bishops' tolerance and, in some cases, their open support of the theological liberalism of the former Bishop of Durham, David Jenkins. On moral issues, he condemns their refusal to give an unambiguous moral condemnation of homosexual sex. He also criticises evangelical leaders for what he perceives to be their acceptance of General Synod and diocesan bureaucratic centralism at the expense of what he insists is the primary structure of the Church's mission, the parish church. For these and other reasons David Holloway believes that the reform of the Church of England will now only come from networks of lay evangelicals and parish clergy, like REFORM, who are prepared, if necessary, to defy central and diocesan authority.

But has Keele failed? And is REFORM justified in threatening schism?

An answer must surely begin by respecting that a final judgment on Keele is impossible so soon after the Congress. Thirty years is hardly a long time in the life of the Church of England, and not a long enough period to expect to make radical changes in a church which by virtue of its history and constitution is so resistant to change by any one party. Indeed to expect radical change to come in so short a period reflects a serious misunderstanding of the nature of the Church of England. An evangelical diocesan bishop recently made this point to me in connection with REFORM when he confided that while the office of bishop may have the appearance of power, in reality it is subject to a host of checks and balances which force him to take the long-term view.

Nevertheless, despite the resistance to change built into church structures, it can be agreed that without Keele the Church of England would be in a far worse state than it is at present. With the collapse of the traditionalists, who tied themselves up in knots over women priests, and the present loss of confidence and poor organisation of the liberals, the evangelicals have stepped in to give the Church of England much-needed support. At a time when statistics warn of a church in terminal decline, it is certainly comforting for all to know that there are many full evangelical churches, that there has been a flowering of evangelical scholarship, that evangelicals have been making a valuable and creative contribution to liturgical development, and that many evangelicals are still putting themselves forward as ordination candidates.

What more can be said for Keele? In particular, can anything more be said to gainsay the view that Keele's apparent success obscures a radical departure from the pure evangelicalism now only represented by REFORM?

To find out, and to shed some light on the gathering crisis linked with REFORM, in the Michaelmas term of 1994 I invited a group of prominent and yet representative evangelicals to a symposium in the University of Durham. This book is the collection of the addresses given at that symposium.

Looking back at Keele

The collection begins with an historical perspective of Keele by Michael Saward. Having been personally involved in drafting the Keele Statement, he is well qualified to take us behind the congress plenaries. His look back at Keele may be especially helpful to the younger generation of Anglican evangelicals, who are possibly unaware of the long history of disagreement within the movement and the impressive way the older generation of evangelical at Keele accepted to agree to disagree for the sake of Christian unity.

The debate over Keele

The second section fleshes out the two sides of the current debate over Keele within Anglican evangelicalism.

David Holloway first puts the case for REFORM. Peter Baron then responds with the case against REFORM.

I have placed these two papers alongside each other with the minimum of editing, for the reason that the truth in this debate is best served by allowing the contestants to fully speak for themselves. However, I am bound to comment that the two papers hardly bear comparison.

David Holloway's is journalistic in style and content, and does not amount to a full treatment of the subject. Nevertheless, in the protest against a bureaucratic centralism that he claims is consuming scarce resources that ought to be deployed in the Church's primary mission field, his case for REFORM deserves a hearing as a cry from the periphery – the parishes, against the centre – the bishops and General Synod.

Peter Baron's contribution is a detailed critique. He claims that REFORM's theological method is stuck in a reaction to modernity and that its understanding of the Church is too narrow and exclusive. His conclusion that REFORM represents the 'last rites of the male, Western, Enlightenment, and privileged sub-culture of Evangelicalism' deserves to be widely pondered.

Keele evangelicals on reform

The third section contains six contributions from mainstream or Keele evangelicals. Each member of this group was asked to give an address on a topic closely related to their sphere of ministry and of key importance to the reform of the Church. In the way 'think tanks' have recently been used to inject fresh ideas into political and economic debate, they were encouraged to 'think the unthinkable'. Their contributions, together with the range of their strategic ministries, give some indication of what Keele evangelicals are contributing and stand poised to contribute in coming years to the reform of the Church of England.

Paying for ministry

Michael Turnbull is Chairman of the Turnbull Commission with responsibility for the reform of the central organisation of the Church, which includes the Church Commissioners. It is a crucial responsibility because the existence of the Commissioners' assets of £2.4 billion and its reported loss, in 1994, of £800 million, is seen by many and, in particular, the poor, as a scandal undermining the integrity of the whole Church of England. As his contribution to the symposium, Michael Turnbull addressed the question whether the Church Commissioners practise an 'option for the poor'.

Training for ministry

John Pritchard as the warden of a Church of England theological college, presents another example of a mainstream evangelical strategically placed to influence reform. He addresses the question of the reform of ministerial training in the light of the recent forced closure of some theological colleges and the perceived failure of present patterns of training.

The ministry of laity

David Day, as an educationalist and a lay reader, is an example
of a Keele evangelical engaging with the mission of the Church
to the University. He very nobly accepted to respond to what
must be the most unpopular issue in the Church of England
after the Archbishop of Canterbury ruled that its discussion at
General Synod was 'unnecessary, unwelcome, untimely, and
unAnglican'; namely, lay presidency of the Eucharist.

The ministry of women

Margaret Masson would doubtless be unhappy with the label
'evangelical' were it not for Keele. As her contribution to the
symposium, she accepted to address the obvious question
following on from the ordination of women to the priesthood:
'And now . . . a woman bishop?'

The ministry of parish clergy

Michael Wilcock, like many of the senior evangelicals who
have made such a success of parish ministry, has devoted a
lifetime to exploring what really matters in parish matters. As
such, he is well qualified to respond to the identity crisis facing
many parish clergy by answering the apparently confusing
question: 'What is a parish priest?'

The ministry of bishops

Ruth Etchells, recently retired, has represented the mainstream
evangelical movement in an impressive lay ministry spanning
the nearly three decades since Keele. As a present member
of the Crown Appointments Commission, she has had the
opportunity to influence the composition of the House of

Bishops. In this role she is well placed to reflect on whether bishops should be elected (as in most other provinces of the Anglican Communion) for a fixed term.

The ministry of cathedrals

The final chapter on the ministry of cathedrals requires a separate introduction, if only to remind evangelicals that they are not the only party concerned with the reform of the Church of England. It is not written by an evangelical. John Arnold is the catholic Dean of Durham. I have included it in this collection for a number of reasons.

For one, it contains part of the Dean's response to the Howe Commission on the reform of cathedrals in which he criticises, as REFORM does, the increasing bureaucratic centralism of the Church of England. For another, expressing all his great love for the beautiful Norman cathedral that adorns the city of Durham, John Arnold explains that 'cathedrals exist to keep open a large view of God and of his goodness and a large view of human potentiality as well as a realistic view of human sinfulness'. Many would agree that this is precisely the view of God and of humanity that Keele attempted to capture for evangelicals, and that REFORM now threatens.

Looking forward to the millennium

In closing this introduction, and in looking forward to all the evangelical party could contribute to the Church of England in the final years of this millennium, it is important to underline the seriousness of the tensions between REFORM and the mainstream or Keele evangelical. As Michael Saward warns, 'a serious collapse in the [evangelical] movement in the last five years of this century cannot be ignored.'

As has happened before, it looks as if the evangelical ascendancy is about to collapse just when it has most to offer the Church of England.

What is there to be done? Two imperatives spring to mind. The first is to exhort all evangelicals to recover the note of repentance struck at Keele. Repentance, especially of the will to power, would help mitigate the already damaging power struggle that is under way between the leaders of REFORM and mainstream evangelical bishops, and might yet provide the will to channel conflict over status, resources and the independence of parish clergy into reforms agreeable to both sides.

The second is to insist, before anyone finally chooses between Keele and REFORM, that all evangelicals take a fresh look at the Keele Statement and decided for themselves whether the spirit of Keele is still worth uniting around. To this end, with the permission of CPAS, the complete Keele Statement is enclosed as Appendix A.

I purposefully use the word 'spirit' above, rather than 'letter', for in the preamble John Stott was careful to note that the Keele Statement must not be taken as 'our last and unalterable word. It is more a beginning than an end'. It is with this insight, that Keele was only the beginning of an Anglican evangelical reformation, that I have included A Basis of Faith for the Anglican Evangelical Assembly as Appendix B. This more recent statement, adopted in the early 1980s, captures much of the spirit of Keele. It will also repay study for those searching for a basis for evangelical unity.

I wish to thank all the contributors for permission to publish, and the Bishop of Guildford, the Rt Revd John Gladwin, for kindly contributing a Foreword.

Charles Yeats
The Castle, Durham
Easter 1995

PART ONE

Looking Back at Keele

Behind the plenaries

Michael Saward

Michael Saward is the Canon Treasurer of St Paul's Cathedral,
and is the author of *Evangelicals on the Move* (1987). He was
personally involved in drafting the Keele Statement.

The Keele Congress of 1967 did not fall pre-packed from the
sky. On the contrary, it was the culmination of nearly fifteen
years of slow but purposeful thinking.

The evangelical culture of the immediate post-war years had
changed little from that of the 1930s when, in the words of
Randle Manwaring, 'evangelicals inclined to the view that they
were excused culture, scholarship, and intellectual exercise on
religious grounds and they felt exonerated from loving God
with their minds. It was all part of their "backs-to-the-wall"
attitude.' This attitude, he affirmed, made them 'a separate
people and their contact with non-Christians was minimal
. . . they contributed little or nothing to political or social
well-being.'[1]

Following my ordination in 1956, I began to attend our
Deanery Clergy Chapter and also our Diocesan Evangelical
Fellowship. My vicar couldn't understand why I bothered to
attend the former, since he and the other local evangelical
incumbent largely ignored it. I found it both irritating and
stimulating but it gave me my first platform to challenge received opinions among its, mostly Anglo-Catholic, members,
concerning the evangelicals. I even tackled the Prolocutor of
the Canterbury Convocation, who came to speak, and who
offered some very dismissive remarks. I very soon came to see
that this 'received opinion' was parroted by large numbers of

clergy who were often incapable of any coherent defence of
it.

How wide open it was to a tough, but friendly, presentation of the evangelical case! And how different from the
Diocesan Evangelical Fellowship. That little group of old men
was defeated, defensive, and dismissive of all attitudes other
than their own essentially sectarian viewpoint. The Church of
England was a body to be attacked or ignored, from the citadel
of parishes with a safe evangelical patronage and the security
of the freehold. I came away from those meetings depressed
by the rigidity of cliché-dominated discussion and backward
thinking.

With hindsight I can see that perhaps the most important
letter (a duplicated one) which came through my front door
at that time was an invitation to join a private, and very
prestigious, society called 'Eclectics'. I jumped at the chance
and attended my first meeting in early 1959. Fresh air, and
great gusts of it. There were just three qualifications required
for nomination. First, acceptance of the supreme authority
of Scripture and, second, a willingness to attend regularly.
Give up on either and you were consigned to outer darkness!
Lastly, you had to be under forty.

The Eclectic Society had originally been founded by John
Newton in 1783 and had quietly foundered in the early nineteenth century. In April 1955 John Stott, Rector of All Souls,
Langham Place, invited twenty-two younger clergy to re-found
the society with him. Year by year numbers grew and, with
each keeping a maximum membership of forty, the groups
had reached seventeen by 1967. Ten years later, in 1977, the
then national chairman, Christopher Byworth, could claim
that Eclectics had included in its membership 'virtually all of
those who are now influential figures in the evangelical wing
of the Church of England'. He was, of course, referring only to
clergy since Eclectics was essentially a clerical meeting point.

To those who were 'Eclectics' in the first fifteen years, the
opportunity provided to discuss, plan, and ultimately reform
the Church of England was exhilarating. The atmosphere was

so radically different from that in the older Diocesan Fellow-ships. *They* grumbled and looked backwards; *we* discussed and planned forwards. A new era was dawning and new leaders were emerging. The old men were in their sixties; the new ones were only in their thirties or early forties. They were to have thirty years of leadership before them.

The early 1960s saw two movements developing which caused tension within the evangelical constituency. The first was associated with a rediscovery of Puritan theology. Two names were dominant: Dr Martyn Lloyd-Jones, Minister of Westminster Chapel, and Dr James Packer, Warden of Latimer House, Oxford. Their influence was supported by the publications of *The Banner of Truth* most of which were heavily subsidised re-issues of Puritan classics (generally run-ning to anything between 500 and 800 pages). The movement increasingly led towards independency and Lloyd-Jones came into open conflict with John Stott at the interdenominational National Evangelical Assembly in October 1966. Stott, chairing the meeting, rejected Lloyd-Jones' call for all evan-gelicals to leave their denominations and create a new 'pure' church. Stott was strongly supported by the *Church of England Newspaper* which called the Lloyd-Jones plea 'nothing short of hare-brained'. Packer and Lloyd-Jones parted company.

The second movement, initially known as 'charismatic', was to cause quite different embarrassment to John Stott. Michael Harper, one of his curates at All Souls, Langham Place, and chaplain to the Oxford Street stores, was 'baptised in the Holy Spirit' (to use the movement's description of the experience of speaking in tongues) and two other All Souls curates fol-lowed him. Hylson-Smith describes what transpired as being viewed by 'evangelicals at large . . . as somewhat bizarre, unwelcome, or even incredible'.[2] Serious divisions began in local congregations where, to many, charismatics were re-garded as 'unsystematic, untheological, and in the last resort, unbiblical'. Nevertheless, the movement grew fast, touching a sympathetic chord already in tune with the youth culture of the 1960s, and the anti-institutionalism which was its trademark.

This last feature was to have its legacy in an ongoing distrust of the institutional life of the Church of England, which remains in many 'renewal' churches even in the mid-1990s.

Meanwhile, Raymond Turvey, Vicar of St George's, Leeds, and some other clergy from the York Province had organised two successful Northern Evangelical Conferences in the early 1960s and from these came the idea of a national congress. Turvey and George Marchant, (later to be Archdeacon of Auckland) with others, met Stott and Peter Johnston, Vicar of Islington, and the Congress took shape following that meeting in May 1964.

The shape of the Congress, as initially conceived, was that there should be eleven addresses, including an opening one from Michael Ramsey, Archbishop of Canterbury, and a closing sermon by Stuart Blanch, Bishop of Liverpool, during the concluding Holy Communion. The nine addresses by selected speakers were each to be approximately one hour in length, and these were to be published following the Congress. All of this was geared to the forthcoming 1968 Lambeth Conference whose theme was the 'Renewal of the Church in Faith, Ministry, and Unity'.

The nine addresses and speakers were, in order of presentation: 'The Good Confession' (Our Crisis and God's Christ), J. I. Packer; 'Jesus Christ our Teacher and Lord' (Authority), J. R. W. Stott; 'The Salvation of Christ' (The Gospel of Grace and Glory), J. Atkinson; 'Christ's Sacrifice and Ours' (Communion and the Cross), E. M. B. Green; 'New Men in Christ' (Law and Love), J. A. Motyer; 'The Credibility of the Church' (Ecumenism), P. E. Hughes; 'Reviving the Local Church' (Body of Christ in Action), W. Leathem; 'Christian Worldliness' (Christian Involvement), J. N. D. Anderson; 'Total Commitment to Christ's Command' (Mission Challenge), A. T. Houghton.

The project, in these terms, had the support of a wide range of evangelical Anglican bodies, including the Church of England Evangelical Council, the Church Pastoral-Aid Society, the Church Society, the Fellowship of Evangelical

Churchmen, and the Federation of Diocesan Evangelical Unions. All were involved in the planning of the Congress, though attendance at committee meetings as the days went by was markedly less evident by those representing the older and more reactionary groups.

Inevitably the overall plan (not being secret) created a strong anxiety among members of the Eclectic Society. The prospect of attending a four-day-long congress and being on the silent, receiving end of eleven lengthy homilies was not an attractive one to those schooled in the cut-and-thrust of debate.

This concern came to a head at the First National Eclectic Conference at Swanwick, in Derbyshire. During the previous eleven years Eclectics had met in groups, and occasional larger conferences, but this was the first full-scale gathering of the whole Society. It met from 14 to 17 November 1966[3] and in the early hours of Thursday 17 – between midnight and 2 a.m. – six of us (Eddie Shirras, Frank Entwhistle, Philip Crowe, George Hoffman, Gavin Reid, and myself) chewed the cud energetically and produced a brief motion for the morning plenary. This, passed almost unanimously, 'resolved to refer to the NEAC (National Evangelical Anglican Congress) sponsoring committee the concern of many members, (a) that NEAC delegates be allowed to contribute as well as listen, and (b) that a document of findings and practical proposals should come out of the Congress, having been prepared in draft beforehand.' The latter suggestion was peculiarly my own as I had, in 1964, attended the British Council of Churches' Faith and Order Conference at Nottingham, where a statement had been debated and produced (which incorporated the famous 'Unity by Easter 1980' proposal).

It seemed absolutely clear to me that Keele would soon be forgotten if something of the kind were not to emerge. Time proved how prescient that judgment was. Keele's statement and, to a lesser extent, Nottingham's ten years later, were both of considerable significance. Caister (NEAC 3), in 1988, set its face against any such document and, of the three NEACs, Caister (with far the largest attendance) made easily the least impact. Only seven years later, it is virtually forgotten. Keele and Nottingham kept the title 'NEAC' as National Evangelical Anglican *Congress* whereas Caister stuck to the acronym but became the National Evangelical Anglican *Celebration*. To be immodest, if I am remembered for anything it ought to be for having had the political judgment to press for that concept of the Statement – that was the tip of Keele's huge iceberg and it tells us precisely where the evangelical movement was in the spring of 1967.

The immediate consequence of that Eclectics' motion was the transformation it created in the agreed goals of the Keele Committee. Gavin Reid had been invited to present the Eclectic proposals to them on 1 December and the minutes indicate how clearly he did it. The Committee agreed 'in principle' to the requests after their having been 'fully discussed'. They went on to invite me to join the Committee and within a few weeks also added George Hoffman and Philip Crowe. The work of the Committee which had a theoretical membership of twenty-three (of whom nineteen were clergy!) was, due to the low attendance of half the members, effectively conducted by eleven members who were, in descending age, Peter Johnston, Raymond Turvey (the Secretary), Roy Cattell, John Stott (the Chairman), James Packer, Timothy Dudley-Smith, myself, Timothy Hoare, Gavin Reid, George Hoffman, and Philip Crowe.

John Stott wrote, that week, to all the Congress speakers informing them of the changes envisaged. The Congress book, *Guidelines*, containing their papers, would be made available to all delegates a week or so before the event and the speakers would be asked to give short expositions, 'hammering home' the main themes and in response to questions from delegates, have a chance to elucidate and clarify specific points.

He went on to introduce the 'Statement' idea which would 'express and apply their themes in terms of policy', and be 'a good public relations document', commanding the 'attention of non-Evangelicals'. The initial draft for discussion at the Congress would be prepared by Gavin Reid, Colin Buchanan and Michael Green, and submitted to Jim Packer and others for assessment.

Additionally, evangelical congregations in over seven hundred parishes had already begun to study an eighteen-week course entitled 'Christ Over All' in order to prepare themselves and their delegates for Keele itself.

A month later, at the annual Islington Clerical Conference, John Stott presented the forthcoming Congress and urged clergy and parishes to put Keele into their planning. He expressed concern over the fact that evangelicals 'have a very poor image in the Church as a whole' with a 'reputation for narrow partisanship and obstructionism' for which, he added, 'we have no one but ourselves to blame'. We need, he went on, 'to repent and to change'. He stressed that he did not see 'evangelical' as a 'party word' and that, in consequence, we 'must take great care . . . that what we are seeking to defend and champion is . . . not some party shibboleth or tradition of doubtful Biblical pedigree'.

And so the Congress took place. A thousand delegates spent four days in discussion, reviewing and amending the draft Statement, in an atmosphere of high enthusiasm and excitement. The sub-plenaries and plenaries were brilliantly chaired by Norman Anderson and John Stott and the sense of the strategic importance of the whole event became almost palpable. Those of us most involved in the behind-the-scenes work were absolutely exhausted, none more so than Philip Crowe and Raymond Turvey, who between them had seen the Statement and the organisation through to completion. For myself, I had the double job of looking after thirty-three Observers and acting as Press Officer. I wasn't to know it, but it was to be a major factor in my being appointed the Archbishop's Radio and Television Officer six months later.

Among the eminent Observers present (who played a full part in debate – though not the voting on the Statement) there was a very enthusiastic response. John Lawrence (an eminent lay member of the Church Assembly) spoke of NEAC as 'a turning point for the whole Church'. He added that he had 'long been convinced that there can be no revival of the Church in this country without the full participation of the evangelicals'. Canon David Paton (Secretary of the Missionary and Ecumenical Council of the Church Assembly) warmly commended the Congress and asked, perceptively, 'have evangelicals fully grasped that to play a real part in the corporate life of the Church of England involves taking very seriously . . . the existence and views of those who are not . . . evangelicals?'

So what had the Congress said in its Statement? The full document appears as an appendix at the end of this book, but it may be useful to add, at this point, a selection of the pieces which were to have especial significance.

The Report (*Keele '67*) and its Statement highlighted six areas of concern under the overall title of 'Christ Over All'. The six were: The Church and its Message (17 clauses); The Church and its Mission (19 clauses); The Church and the World (16 clauses); The Church and its Structures (11 clauses); The Church and its Worship (17 clauses); The Church and its Unity (22 clauses).

In selecting representative paragraphs it is quite impossible to do justice to the Report and, in general, I have omitted both doctrinal statements which are obvious and unexceptional and items which were particularly dated to issues of the day (e.g. the Anglican–Methodist proposals). I have, however, specifically included matters which directly relate to ongoing areas of dispute. The paragraph numbers are those used in the Report itself.

The Church and its message

1. We affirm our belief in the historic faith of the Church, in an age in which it has come under attack from both outside and inside the Church.

5. Revelation is by word as well as by deed. God reveals Himself not only in mighty acts but also in the word by

which He interprets those acts. We therefore receive the Bible as authoritative divine teaching, and conclude that to differ from the Bible is to deviate from the truth.

6. Scripture is the supreme authority in all matters of faith and practice both for the Church and for the individual. It is also the means of grace through which God reveals Himself in present experience.

    We affirm that the supreme agent of biblical interpretation is the Holy Spirit, who directs Christians in their search to understand the message of God. This message was given through the minds of the biblical writers, and must be considered in relation to their personal, social, and national situations. We welcome all scholarship which promotes a more precise understanding of holy Scripture. Thus we confess our faith that the Scriptures are the wholly trustworthy oracles of God.

11. Whereas God in the gospel commands all men to repent and believe and offers salvation freely to all who do, not all men accept His grace. Scripture has no place for a universal salvation, or for the possibility of a further successful probation in a future life for those who reject Christ in this. A persistent and deliberate rejection of Jesus Christ condemns men to hell.

14. We thank God for creating in us a hunger to seek the best gifts of the Spirit in fullest possible measure, and we rejoice at every sign of His working in human lives. In this connection however, we have no united opinion as to whether current 'charismatic' manifestations are of the same sort as the corresponding New Testament 'gifts of the Spirit' or not.

The Church and its mission

18. Mission originates in the nature of God. It is the activity by which He works to restore the world to harmony with Himself. It is the work of God the Father, who is

always active in saving love and in judgment within His rebellious world. It is the work of God the Son, in whom God has reconciled the world to Himself, and through whom alone men are redeemed. It is the work of God the Spirit, who testifies to the world of God's redeeming love, and by His recreative action brings sinful men to know Christ personally and to find in Him new life.

19. God graciously calls the Church to share in His mission, and all Christians are involved in this calling.

20. God's purpose is to make men new through the gospel, and through their transformed lives to bring all aspects of human life under the Lordship of Christ. Christians share in God's work of mission by being present among non-Christians to live and to speak for Christ, and in His name to promote justice and meet human need in all its forms. Evangelism and compassionate service belong together in the mission of God.

27. The missionary situation in many parts of Britain, particularly in industrial inner-city and new housing areas, calls for special action. We have to admit to our shame that the Church has so far largely failed these areas.

   We urge that dioceses will designate special mission areas, calling for support from the wider Church, and the maximum flexibility in matters of organisation and liturgy.

28. We affirm the unique claims of Jesus Christ to be the only Saviour, through whom alone men can be saved, and deprecate the current tendency to equate all religions as ways which eventually lead to God. We welcome sympathetic dialogue with their adherents, but we reject as misleading the statement that Christ is already present in other faiths. We cannot regard those true insights which non-Christian religions contain as constituting a way of salvation.

The Church and the world

38. This is God's world in spite of its invasion by evil. He cares for it and so must we. The Church is set in the world by God Himself, who has made us both citizens of our country and ambassadors for Christ. We must therefore work not only for the redemption of individuals, but also for the reformation of society.

42. In regard to abortion, we judge that the life of the mother and her physical and mental health, must have priority over the potential personality of the foetus. We therefore urge that questions such as alleged rape, the possibility that the embryo might be malformed, and social considerations, should not be regarded as grounds for abortion unless the mother's health is in danger.

49. We affirm that all mankind is one in the sight of God. We therefore condemn racial discrimination in all countries and are especially concerned at the appearance of it in our own country in the spheres of employment and accommodation. We support all constructive policies and efforts to improve relations between groups and individuals of different races.

50. Many parts of the world are already over populated; and hunger, poverty and starvation are widespread.

We are concerned that in some nations ignorance, superstition, or even religious beliefs are obstacles both to the fullest use of food resources, and to the control of population. We believe that God has entrusted to man the responsibility for controlling procreation, and we hold that contraception is morally right when responsibly used.

51. We assert that marriage is the divinely ordained state in which complete sexual fulfilment is to be sought. Pre-marital and extra-marital intercourse are therefore contrary to this principle and are responsible for much unhappiness.

52. We are deeply concerned about all forms of addiction

in this country today and in particular that of drug
addiction. The position is so grave that we also call for
funds to provide more centres, and we encourage pilot
schemes for rehabilitation of addicts.

The Church and its structures

53. The Church is one people. The difference between clergy
    and laity is one of function. Ordination is a calling and
    gift of Christ by His Spirit in His Church, which sets a
    man apart to the ministry of the Word and Sacraments
    and of pastoral care. He is therein given authority and
    power so to minister, but his status is not otherwise
    altered. Ministry is to be exercised by the whole people
    of God, and this must be seen in the life of the Church
    at both local and national level.

55. We call for more co-operation between parishes. We
    have no desire to perpetuate a spirit of isolationism,
    although we submit that group and team ministries create
    special difficulties when there are deep theological differ-
    ences. We commend the idea of voluntary groupings to
    parishes, even where such theological differences exist,
    with a view to greater fellowship and the pooling of
    resources. We recognise that we could well benefit in this
    way from others of a different theological persuasion.
    But we ask that those drawing up schemes for group
    and team ministries under the Pastoral Measure should
    take full account of conscientious doctrinal convictions
    held by the clergy and laity of the parishes involved.

58. We welcome the prospect of clergy and laity serving
    together on an equal basis in Synods.

The Church and its worship

65. We have failed to maintain the unity of Word and Sacrament. While rightly exalting preaching, we have underrated the evangelical function of the sacrament of the Lord's Supper as a visible word. We have been suspicious of experimentation and frightened of change, and have tended to individualism. Furthermore, we have been slow to learn from other parts of God's Church.

66. Local variations in worship should not cause Christians to take offence when they move from one part of the country to another. Equally, local churches should not give offence by unlawful innovations. We call on all local churches to abide by the present law, even where it seems irksome. We ourselves will seek reform only by lawful means.

69. We call on the Church to set the highest standards for the ministry of the Word, to proclaim the whole counsel of God, and to recover an eager expectation of receiving grace through this means. Preaching is the authoritative proclamation of the Word of God, applied by the Spirit, demanding decision rather than discussion. We therefore regard the development of techniques of discussion and dialogue for Christian instruction as a useful adjunct to preaching, but not as a substitute for it.

71. Baptism is the sign and seal of covenant-relationship between God and His people.

   We affirm our belief in the scriptural foundation of infant baptism, but declare that only the children of parents who profess to be Christians are fit subjects for this rite. Indiscriminate infant baptism as commonly practised in England, is a scandal, and is incidentally productive of much of the current divisive reaction against the baptising of infants. We call now for a theologically-inspired national practice of baptismal discipline.

72. We urge that baptism should always be held at public

services of the Church, unless there are compelling reasons to the contrary.

75. We reject rebaptism as unscriptural. It is destructive of the sacrament, makes it a sign of our faith rather than of God's grace, and removes its once-for-all character. It is also hurtful to the unity of God's people.

76. We have failed to do justice in our practice to the twin truths that the Lord's Supper is the main service of the people of God, and that the local church, as such, is the unit within which it is properly administered. This is not to undervalue in any way attendance at other services of the day, but to admit that we have let the sacrament be pushed to the outer fringes of Church life, and the ministry of the Word be divorced from it.

    We determine to work towards the practice of a weekly celebration of the sacrament as the central corporate service of the Church.

79. We welcome the continuing growth of family worship as the liturgical threshold by which whole families are introduced to the life of the Church, and thus to Jesus Christ.

    Non-sacramental family services must not, however, become ends in themselves, but must lead on to participation in the full worship of the Church, including the sacraments.

The Church and its unity

81. God's Church is one, as God is one. This oneness is God's gift to those who obey the gospel. It finds its proper expression when all the Christians of a locality appear as a single visible fellowship, united in truth and holiness, displayed in love, service and worship (especially at the Lord's Supper), and active in evangelism. The Church is to show its given oneness in order that the world may believe. We cannot now rest content with a profession of

being one in Christ with all believers if that profession
becomes an excuse for refusing to seek local organic
unity. We therefore not only reaffirm the general profession, but pledge ourselves to seek this specific goal.

83. A dialogue is a conversation in which each party is
serious in his approach both to the subject and to the
other person, and desires to listen and learn as well
as to speak and instruct. The initial task for divided
Christians is dialogue, at all levels and across all barriers.
We desire to enter this ecumenical dialogue fully. We
are no longer content to stand apart from those with
whom we disagree. We recognise that all who 'confess
the Lord Jesus Christ as God and Saviour according to
the Scriptures and therefore seek to fulfil together their
common calling to the glory of the one God, Father,
Son and Holy Spirit' (World Council of Churches' Basis)
have a right to be treated as Christians, and it is on that
basis that we wish to talk with them.

84. This does not mean that we think all points of
view equally valid or all theological and ecclesiastical
systems equally pleasing to God. It means only that
we, who know ourselves to be prone to error and
infected by sin, wish to join in conversation with
others who are similarly affected, yet who profess
to know God's grace, as we do. The aim is that
together we may learn from the Bible what God by
His Spirit has to say to us all.

Polemics at long range have at times in the past led us
into negative and impoverishing 'anti-' attitudes (anti-
sacramental, anti-intellectual, etc.), from which we now
desire to shake free. We recognise that in dialogue we
may hope to learn truths held by others to which we
have hitherto been blind, as well as to impart to others
truths held by us and overlooked by them.

85. We do not suppose that Evangelicals have a monopoly
of the Spirit's ministry in this regard. Through dialogue,
therefore, we look to God to instruct and reform us all.

86.   Dialogue and reformation should start at home. The chaos in doctrinal matters in the Church of England today causes us grief and shame. We reject the current tendency towards 'Christian agnosticism' over the fundamentals of the gospel. In the face of this situation, however, it is reform that we desire, not separation.

87.   We are deeply committed to the present and future of the Church of England. We believe that God has led us to this commitment, and we dare to hope and pray that through it God will bring His Word to bear with new power upon this Church. We do not believe secession to be a live issue in our present situation.

88.   Our basic loyalty is to the Word of God and the people of God. While we accept that in England episcopacy seems the only pattern for reunion, we do not believe that it is a theological necessity.

89.   The Lord's Supper is the focus of the Church's unity.

90.   For good order the Church should appoint its officers to preside at the Supper, but there is no scriptural warrant for insisting that these must be bishops or episcopally ordained presbyters.

96.   We recognise that the Roman Catholic Church holds many fundamental Christian doctrines in common with ourselves. We rejoice also at signs of biblical reformation. While we could not contemplate any form of reunion with Rome as she is, we welcome the new possibilities of dialogue with her on the basis of Scripture.

The Keele Statement was not, and is not, an infallible document. In his Introduction, John Stott wisely pointed out that it 'must not be regarded as binding on the mind, conscience or action of any of the individuals present or of the churches and societies they may have represented . . . it does not claim to be more than the consensus of the great majority' expressing 'the convictions of a large but average evangelical constituency'. The Statement, he concluded, 'must not be taken as our last and unalterable word. It is more a beginning than an end.' So, he commended it not only for study but 'study with a view to action'.

A few days after the Congress concluded, the *Church of England Newspaper* in its editorial report commented that 'for the first time in a generation representative Evangelicals have come together to hammer out the refractory issues which we must all face if we are to do our Christian duty in 1967. It is a great achievement to have got so far. We must now go on to possess the land which has been opened up before us. The Congress Statement is a charter and a programme for us all.'

Surprisingly, perhaps, the *English Churchman* (which was a small circulation paper and a sometimes harsh critic of much in the Anglican evangelical world) announced that 'only the highest praise can be given to those responsible'.

What were the consequences of Keele? In my judgment there were at least four main results which are so evident a quarter of a century later as hardly to need stating.

The numerical growth of the movement

This is self-evident, especially in terms of the growth of ordinands who are the Church of the future's seed-corn. Year by year the percentage of male ordinands in the evangelical theological colleges moved up one or one-and-a-half points until by the late 1980s the figure was well over 50 per cent. By 1993 this figure has reached 56 per cent, as compared with 27 per cent in 'Central' colleges and 17 per cent in Anglo-Catholic colleges. Women ordinands in the evangelical colleges in 1993 had reached 58.3 per cent. Those in Central colleges were 39.1 per cent and in Anglo-Catholic ones 2.5 per cent.

Growth can also be identified with regard to the hierarchy. The total in 1967 was a tiny handful. By 1987 there were seven diocesan bishops, seven suffragans, three deans, and thirteen archdeacons. At the beginning of 1995 these figures had risen to thirteen, thirteen, eight, and twenty respectively. The interpretation of 'evangelical' in these figures is, however, perhaps over-generous. Even so, the growth is from thirty to fifty-four in eight years.

A further area in which growth has been obvious has been within the world of General Synod, Church Commissioners, and related bodies. In this field the growth has been more in terms of the holders of influential offices. In the late 1980s, half the elected Church Commissioners were evangelicals, as were half the elected members of the Crown Appointments Commission.

The intellectual development of the movement

The quality of evangelical scholarship has improved out of all recognition. This is evident in Universities, in publications, in General Synod speeches and in the number of doctoral students who identify with the movement. This whole area is not so easy to quantify but the facts are obvious enough. In the area of biblical and theological studies, and their ethical consequences, the exponents are respected scholars within their fields, grappling with questions that few of their predecessors could have coped with in the 1940s and 1950s.

One mark of the movement's capacity to grapple with theological ideas was the creation, in the early 1980s, of a Basis of Faith for the newly constituted Anglican Evangelical Assembly. This, cast in a fresh format, is a comprehensive, but brief, statement of the movement's doctrinal stance. Nothing comparable has been produced in the twentieth century. The speed with which it was prepared, evaluated, and adopted across the evangelical Anglican world, spoke well for the movement's capacity to think in coherent theological terms. (See Appendix B, p. 214).

The liturgical development of the movement

Evangelicals in the years before Keele were, for the most part, not even vaguely interested in liturgy. They used the Book of Common Prayer, often in a very wooden and unimaginative manner and knew little or nothing about the history and development of liturgy. Because of the battles in the 1920s they maintained themselves to be the only 'Prayer Book men' and defended it most tenaciously (even though they omitted the bits that they didn't like and ignored lectionaries if they felt like it). They had a far higher view of extempore prayer meetings than of services of Holy Communion.

This situation changed rapidly in the 1960s and 1970s. Keele cautiously welcomed modern liturgies and by the late 1970s half the members of the Revision Committee which presented Rite A to the General Synod were evangelicals and they succeeded in creating a widely accepted eucharistic rite which they did not regard as having compromised the evangelical position at any of the essential tension points. At the popular level the development of Grove Booklets, initially in the liturgical field, opened up a new vista to a new generation of younger clergy. From being the reactionaries, evangelicals became the vanguard, though the popular desire for immediacy in worship undermined much of this development in the late 1980s.

The structural development of the movement

By the middle 1960s it was already clear that some of the inherited organisational structures were well past their 'sell by' date. The creation of the Church of England Evangelical Council in 1960, by John Stott, had been an attempt to bring evangelical leaders together to enable them to seek a common mind and to share their convictions with both Church and nation. It became, in due course, the English branch of the Evangelical Fellowship in the Anglican Communion and in the early 1980s created the Anglican Evangelical Assembly, as an annual focus for the constituency. CEEC, sadly, has never been able to gain the trust of the whole range, being viewed with extreme caution by the 'hard right' members of the Church Society, and with indifference by the various charismatic groups. It remains the voice-piece of the mainstream but, sadly, has gradually lost credibility due to its unwillingness, or inability, to make public statements on subjects concerning which the constituency has expected at least an opinion from it. The ordination of women to the priesthood was the supreme example of this failure.

Attempts in the 1960s and 1970s to unify some of the inherited societies (which was widely desired) all failed. Large conferences in the 1960s had voted, almost unanimously, for a merger between the Church Pastoral-Aid Society and the Church Society, but neither society (both run by unrepresentative cabals) would contemplate giving up its autonomy. Similar attempts at more unified missionary society structures were equally unproductive. Finally after a long battle in the 1970s the Church Pastoral-Aid Society reformed its whole constitutional and electoral procedures and the Society's role has hugely advanced in the succeeding years. Fortunately, the work among children and young people had been transferred from Church Society to Church Pastoral-Aid Society in 1975 which saved it from what might well have been complete collapse and opened it up to tremendous growth and progress, reaching out into previously unimagined areas within the wider Church of England. Today the CPAS youth organisations (known by the acronym CYPECS) are probably the largest and most effective teaching and evangelising agencies among the young within the national Church.

If these four consequences (and there were others) were evident marks of advance in the following two decades what other factors existed which militated against the fulfilment of Keele's hopes?

Far and away the most powerful and two-edged influence was the growth of the charismatic or 'renewal' movement. To those who were not caught up in it, the claim to be the 'renewal' people was mildly offensive since others believed that they had more than contributed to the renewal of the Church in quite different ways. Nevertheless, the worldwide development of the movement across a wide range of churches, far removed from the 'evangelical' mainstream, undoubtedly brought a new vitality to countless congregations and individuals. Much of the old starchiness went out of church life. The recognition of widespread 'giftedness' was to release many from the clergy-centred concepts which had gone before. There were, in short, many gains to be acknowledged.

Nevertheless, when the histories come to be written it may well be seen that the charismatic influence was at least as damaging as it was beneficial within the evangelical Anglican movement. For the most part, those involved, while seeing numerical growth in their congregations, became increasingly isolated from the actual renewal of the Church of England at almost every level outside parish life. 'Renewal' people generally were not prepared to bother with deaneries, dioceses, synods, indeed with the institutional life of the Church. There were, of course, some notable exceptions to this, but, as a rule of thumb, where 'renewal' dominated, thoughtful strategic thinking and acting for the good of the structured life of the Church of England was regrettably absent. Charismatic leaders were noticeably missing from the Church of England Evangelical Council and rarely seen at the annual Anglican Evangelical Assemblies. An attempt at rapprochement between the mainstream and the charismatics was partially successful in the years preceding the second NEAC at Nottingham and led to the publication of a short monograph, 'Gospel and Spirit'[4] and the participation of some leading charismatics at Nottingham; but the self-isolation of the average local charismatic from mainstream evangelical Anglican and official Church of England events was hardly affected and the drift continued throughout the 1980s and early 1990s.

One significant element in this was the contrast in the field of hymns and songs for worship. The mainstream had been the source and proving ground for the spate of hymns, psalm paraphrases, carols, canticles, prayers, and a 'dramatised'

Bible all emanating from Jubilate Hymns, a group who worked together throughout the whole post-Keele period, providing material that was largely geared to worship of a liturgical or semi-liturgical kind. Much of their material was ignored by charismatic groups and churches who preferred to use songs and choruses of a repetitive kind. Some of these were excellent 'worship songs', well able to be used to enhance Anglican worship. The vast majority were poorly written, set to banal music, and in charismatic churches were often the spearhead used to push liturgy into the background or even out of the building altogether. As the 1980s moved into the 1990s so the number of charismatic churches in the evangelical tradition which had ditched coherent liturgy for 'chorus-sandwiches' grew and grew. As one critic put it, referring to the use of sung choruses during the administration of Holy Communion, 'we use music during Holy Communion, they have Holy Communion during music'.'

It was almost certainly the growth of a theologically unsophisticated 'renewal' tradition in the 1970s and early 1980s that led to the hostile reaction from the Protestant and Puritan end of the evangelical spectrum. This probably began in the late 1970s with a claim from Dick Lucas, Rector of St Helen's Bishopsgate, in the City of London, since 1961, that the evangelical movement was facing an 'identity crisis' and he launched attacks on both Keele and the charismatics. Increasingly, St Helen's, a large and powerful church, has been the focus for anti-mainstream, and anti-renewal, clarion calls although some of that congregation would not endorse such a standpoint. A more recent development from that stable has been the Proclamation Trust, an organisation urging upon its many clerical devotees the need to spend the major part of their time and energy in preparing and preaching expository sermons on biblical passages and texts. The Trust's conferences have, however, included platform attacks on those evangelical groups and individuals who do not find favour with the leadership.

Running in parallel to such criticisms has been the vocal

Church Society, especially during the era of 1983–91 when David Samuel was the Society's Director. The Society (which had been part of the evangelical mainstream until the 1970s) was perceived to have been taken over by a group of old-fashioned Protestant militants who sacked the editor of their respected theological journal, *Churchman*, and precipitated the creation of *Anvil* by the mainstream to continue the tradition. Since then the Church Society, declining in influence, has not been enthusiastic about disclosing the size of *Churchman*'s circulation and its stance has perceptibly shifted to the Protestant and theologically ultra-conservative end of the evangelical spectrum.

It was from these groups that hostility towards Keele first emerged. Roger Beckwith, a lifelong traditionalist, attempted to smear Keele by describing its architects as 'certain young activists of unconventional views' (not mentioning that he was of the same generation) and implying that the older speakers, 'men of some maturity', would not have wished to see the resulting Statement. In fact, at least half of these were enthusiastic advocates and only one, as far as I know, ever publicly questioned, not Keele itself, but the direction in which the movement was travelling in the post-Keele years. That one was James Packer who wrote a wise and thoughtful monograph 'The Evangelical Anglican Identity Problem' in 1978. In it, while recognising changes of style, spirituality, and ethics, and noting that opinions were often divided on these, he saw the root issue as one concerning doctrine. Evangelicals were divided and faced an identity problem because the Church of England itself was unsettled, more particularly because of the influence of 'modernist' and 'radical' theology and the secularist climate of the day. Packer saw the vital need for evangelicals to keep the pressure on bishops to exercise a proper discipline where 'incorrigible heretics' declined to accept episcopal rebuke and he welcomed a pamphlet published by the Church of England Evangelical Council in 1978 *Truth, Error and Discipline in the Church* which had encouraged bishops to withdraw Licences and Permissions in such cases.

Three other matters need a brief comment. The crucial

point of the Caister NEAC in 1988 was when Robert Runcie urged upon evangelicals the need to produce a 'developed evangelical ecclesiology'. If, he added, the current evangelical renewal 'is to have a lasting impact, then there must be more explicit attention given to the doctrine of the church'. John Stott responded, in his Report on Caister, affirming evangelicals' loyalty to the Church of England but recognising that their tendency had been to focus on 'the concepts of an invisible and mystical body' and 'local, independent congregations' at 'the expense of an organised and visible society united by baptism and eucharist'. Since Caister the issue has kept re-emerging and one major book (Timothy Bradshaw's *The Olive Branch*[5]) has placed the item on the agenda even more firmly. Even so, by 1995, the constituency was divided between those who saw the doctrine of the Church as a primary, credal, doctrine and those whose interdenominational sympathies reduced it to a second level of importance.

This second group was created primarily as a response to the decision to ordain women as presbyters (or priests). This decision, welcomed by the majority of evangelical Anglicans, had taken most of them by surprise and they founded REFORM, whose chief goals seemed to be opposition to women priests, existing church structures, and the House of Bishops. A somewhat mixed group, they played the traditional evangelical hand of claiming the moral and theological high ground and ignoring the arguments of the mainstream. Since the greatest weakness historically of the whole evangelical movement has been its tendency to tear itself apart into conflicting groups, and to distrust 'them' (whoever they are) in positions of institutional responsibility, combined with unreal expectations of what can be achieved in a national Church, the danger of a serious collapse in the movement in the last five years of the century cannot be ignored.

It was in order to combat such a disastrous prospect that I invited a group of nine people to meet at my home on 30 March 1994. Having been on the planning committees of all three NEACs, at almost all the Anglican Evangelical Assemblies since their foundation, and a member of the Church of England Evangelical Council from 1976 to 1993, I did not feel it entirely inappropriate to take such an initiative. As one of Roger Beckwith's so-called 'young activists', I felt it time to become, at the age of sixty-one, an 'old activist', and thus become worthy of being later described by Beckwith as 'a minor dignitary'.

The nine people were Bishops Michael Baughen, Roy Williamson, Michael Turnbull, Gavin Reid, Michael Nazir-Ali, Michael Bunker (Dean of Peterborough), Mrs Jill Dann, Archdeacon Gordon Kuhrt, Canon John Moore (General Director of CPAS) who, together with myself, agreed to plan the Evangelical Anglican Leaders' Conference for January 1995.

Writing this chapter before the Conference takes place, I cannot pre-judge how effective it will be, but I am encouraged by some words of greeting from John Stott who hopes for 'more humble, patient, reciprocal listening, which alone could first diagnose and then begin to prescribe remedies for, our current evangelical Anglican malaise'.

The last word, for the moment, shall be with one of the brightest luminaries among younger evangelicals, Dr Alister McGrath. Speaking in November 1994 at the Senior Evangelical Anglican Clergy Conference, he complimented the 300 participants (all of an older generation). 'We are,' he said, speaking on behalf of 'those younger than I am . . . profoundly grateful to you, for all you have done in establishing such a good base for us to work on . . . without what you did we should not be able to face the future with any kind of confidence at all. It is a tribute to your faithfulness that today things seem to be so much better. That really needs,' he concluded, 'to be said.'

I am a realist about the capacity of evangelicals throughout history to disintegrate at the crucial moments. They have done it four times in 400 years and they are more than capable of a fifth successive fiasco. God willing, they might just learn in time.

PART TWO

The Debate Over Keele

The case for REFORM

David Holloway

David Holloway, Vicar of Jesmond in the Diocese of
Newcastle, was for many years a member of General Synod,
is acknowledged as an expert on church growth, and is a
founder member of REFORM.

Hooker and Tertullian

In discussing the reform of the Church of England there are
two warnings to bear in mind. The first is a warning from
Richard Hooker, the Anglican Reformer, at the end of the
sixteenth century. Here are the opening words of his *Laws of
Ecclesiastical Polity*:

> He that goeth about to persuade a multitude, that they
> are not so well governed as they ought to be, shall
> never want attentive and favourable hearers; because
> they know the manifold defects whereunto every kind of
> regiment is subject, but the secret lets and difficulties,
> which in public proceedings are innumerable and inevit-
> able, they have not ordinarily the judgment to consider.

The second and related warning comes from Tertullian, the
Latin Father, much earlier at the end of the second century. He
warned against listening to any theological discussion unless
you know the spiritual pedigree of the writer. He said:

> We admit no man to any disputation concerning sacred
> things, or to the scanning and examining of particular

questions of religion, unless he first show us of whom he received the faith, by whose means he became a Christian, and whether he admit and hold the general principles wherein all Christians do, and ever did, agree.

It is necessary, therefore, to say something about my own pilgrimage and pedigree. At this time of crisis in the Church of England, it is vital that those who analyse and make suggestions should at least be aware of the 'secret lets and difficulties' that the Church has to face and so not be unrealistic in any proposals or criticism.

Background

I write as a 'mainstream evangelical'. This is to follow the categorisation of the *English Church Census* of 1989 that identified evangelicals as 'broad', 'mainstream' or 'charismatic'.

The key influences on my spiritual pilgrimage, apart from family influences, would be a North London evangelical rector in the late 1950s and early 1960s; the OICCU (the Christian Union at Oxford) about the same period with men like John Stott, Jim Packer, Michael Green and Basil Gough as regular visitors; the teaching in the Oxford School of Theology in the early 1960s of men like George Caird, John Baker (later Bishop of Salisbury), Henry Chadwick and V. A. Demant; and also my own chaplain at University College, T. M. Parker – an Anglo-Catholic, a polymath, but with a profound distaste for theological liberalism. He made it conspicuously clear that thoughtfulness and liberalism were not synonymous. Since then other influences have come from working with the Church Missionary Society in the Sudan among Muslim Northerners and Christian Southerners; studying at Ridley Hall, Cambridge, in the 'radical' 1960s (and in reaction being totally convinced of 'mere' or credal Christianity); serving at St George's, Leeds, with its students and its 'Crypt' for the socially inadequate; teaching (theology and ethics) at Wycliffe

Hall, Oxford; and being Vicar of Jesmond, Newcastle upon Tyne.

Over the past twenty-two years I have been privileged to minister at Jesmond Parish Church regularly to hundreds of people, many of whom are young. I have seen a congregation grow over that period and have learnt, I believe, something about what helps and hinders church growth. I have endeavoured to supplement that learning process by studies at Fuller Seminary, in the USA.

With regard to the wider Church of England, I spent fifteen years on the General Synod. For ten of those I was on the Board for Social Responsibility; for five on the General Synod's Standing Committee, its Policy Sub-committee and its Joint Budget Committee. I have been a chairman of the General Synod, a deputy prolocutor, and on various working parties and other committees; also a non-voting member of many deanery synods in my own diocese; and was a member of the Diocesan Board of Finance longer than I like to remember.

I trust, therefore, that what follows is not written without an awareness of genuine problems – the 'secret lets and difficulties' – of the Church of England both at the centre and in the parish. I am aware that for some problems there are no easy answers. But not all problems in the Church are of that sort.

I want to develop my case for reform by setting out a series of assumptions.

First, I am assuming a goal for all of us in the Church, but especially for those in leadership. This is given by St Paul in his letter to the Colossians (1:28–9):

We proclaim him [Jesus Christ], admonishing and teaching everyone with all wisdom, so that we may present everyone perfect [or, better, 'mature'] in Christ. To this end I labour, struggling with all his energy, which so powerfully works in me.

That is to say, there needs to be a ministry of the Word that is both negative and positive – 'admonishing and teaching'; a ministry of the *whole* gospel not just part of it – 'with *all* wisdom'; a ministry involving both effort and conflict – 'labour' and 'struggling'; but a ministry in the strength of the Holy Spirit – 'with all his energy, which so powerfully works in me'. The aim of such ministry is to help people become what God intends them to become – 'mature in Christ'.

My *second* assumption is that the nation is adrift spiritually and in need of evangelising. To that end the Church needs to be reformed. More and more the words of Isaiah of Jerusalem seem so relevant (1:4):

> Ah, sinful nation, a people loaded with guilt, a brood of evildoers, children given to corruption! They have forsaken the Lord.

The nation

Nationally and culturally we are moving beyond post-Modernism to 'post-Christianism'. We now have the first 'post-Christian' generation – these are people in their twenties. The YMCA in a recent survey discovered that two-thirds of the young people interviewed had *never* been to a church. Significantly, some of this generation are now quite open about their helplessness; and they are recognising their needs. One secular writer, Douglas Coupland, in his book *Life After God* concludes:

> My secret is that I need God – that I am sick and can no longer make it alone. I need God to help me give, because I no longer seem to be capable of giving: to help me be kind, as I no longer seem capable of kindness; to help me love, as I seem beyond being able to love.[1]

Even more importantly, there is a growing consensus that

for a society to be healthy it needs health in three critical areas – in its political order, in its economic order but also in its spiritual order. Society is like a three-legged stool: all legs are necessary for the stool to stand upright.

The West, and now the rest of the world, has generally accepted that a form of democratic capitalism is the least worst form of political and economic order. But spiritually there is a vacuum in the West in our public squares. No longer are ruling elites supporting the Judaeo-Christian spiritual tradition. But without the values of that tradition democratic capitalism will lead, and is already leading, to licence, selfish greed, degeneracy and social instability. Such a state of affairs is alarming. There is the risk of it giving birth to tyranny of one sort or another as a means of social control. The threat would come from totalitarian fascism or totalitarian socialism. Either would be unmitigated disasters.

Our world and nation are at a watershed. That is the context of the need to reform the Church. Our society is becoming spiritually bankrupt.

Of course, we need to reform the Church for the effective preaching of the gospel because the gospel is true. We desperately need those three 'R's of evangelical religion – *ruin, redemption* and *regeneration*. They are as relevant today as ever. They remind us that the world is in a mess through rejecting God; Jesus Christ and his cross are the only ultimate answers to that mess; and unless the Holy Spirit makes men and women new, giving them new life through a new birth, there will be no change. There are, indeed, eternal consequences (we need to know of the reality of hell and Jesus Christ as our Saviour from it).

But there are also present consequences from rejecting the gospel. These are worked out in the social order.

* & also CREATION

Pannenberg

Professor Wolfhart Pannenberg, the German theologian, in his 1994 Erasmus Lecture put it like this:

> There are compelling reasons for Western Societies to try to recover their religious roots . . . Given alternative religious possibilities Western Societies are well advised to recover their religious roots in a cultural tradition informed by Jewish and Christian beliefs. Western ideas of human rights and especially the underlying conception of human freedom have their basis in these beliefs: in the Christian teaching that the individual person is the object of God's eternal love and that human freedom has its source in the individual's communion with God through faith, and in the Jewish understanding of the dignity of the human person as created in the image of God. In the light of these teachings, individual freedom cannot be unbridled licence.

He then went on to speak about the acids of secularism:

> Secularism's greatest success, however, is in the widespread demoralisation in the ranks of the clergy and theologians who are supposed to proclaim and interpret the truth of the gospel but delude themselves that they are achieving that purpose by adapting Christian faith and life to the demands of secularism. What the situation requires, I am convinced, is precisely the opposite of such uncritical adaptations. The further secularism advances the more urgent it is that Christian faith and Christian life be seen in sharp contrast to the secular culture . . . What is needed is a strong reaffirmation of the central articles of Christian faith against the spirit of secularism and then a joining of that to a renewed commitment to rationality and ecumenical openness. Needless to say, such a combination is not easy.

The nation is adrift spiritually and in need of evangelising.

The Church of England

My *third* assumption is that the Church of England is adrift doctrinally, morally and in terms of social significance. It is adrift, in part, because its leadership has adapted the Christian faith and life to these demands of secularism.

Doctrinally the Church has drifted from the apostolic faith and its theological roots in the Bible, the 39 Articles and the Book of Common Prayer. Many are now awash in a sea of relativism and multi-faithism. The pluralism of the House of Bishops of the Church of England was evident in their response to the saga of the previous Bishop of Durham, David Jenkins. In their official report, *The Nature of Christian Belief*,[2] they made it clear that to deny the empty tomb of Jesus was acceptable. The empty tomb was *an expression* of the doctrine of the Church of England. The logic (and undoubted intention) of their statement was to allow the denial of the empty tomb also as a legitimate expression of the Church's belief.

I realised just how sick the Church of England was during the General Synod debate at York on that report from the bishops.

The Bishop of Durham had been called to speak. After significant criticism of him following the fire at York Minster and his all too public doubts and denials of the virginal conception and empty tomb of Jesus, it was something of a rehabilitation. It was a 're-entry' after a period of marginalisation. He made an emotional and impassioned speech; and in an obvious allusion to the gospel miracles he made a reference to a God of 'the divine laser beam type of miracle' as being 'a cultic idol' or 'the very devil'. This was very offensive to some in the Synod and many outside. But at the end of his speech there was great applause. Members began to rise. One evangelical bishop, undoubtedly a Keele supporter, was on his feet clapping away and seeming to lead the applause. Then hundreds of members, bishops, clergy and laity, rose to their feet.

Group pressure

A parallel came to mind. It was from the first 'moving picture'
I ever saw. In one scene people were clapping, standing and
cheering. They were respectable, good-looking people; and
there were thousands of them. Then the camera panned round
to the object of their applause. It was Adolph Hitler. The film
was of the Berlin 1936 Olympic Games.

I was aware at the Synod, as never before, of group
pressure in the Church. It was frightening. I could understand
perfectly how it was that so many seemingly good Christians
in Germany, between the wars, failed to identify with the
Confessing Church; instead they were numbered among
the pro-Nazi German Christians and thus validated all the
atrocities that went on under the name of National Socialism.

The parallel with evangelicals in the Church of England,
especially those in high office, was clear. It is so easy to
lose your roots, your views and your values when immersed
week by week, month by month in structures that are no
longer the biblical and apostolic ones of your evangelical
youth, but are neo-gnostic, neo-Arian, and neo-deist. This
indeed is the colour of the new 'lowest common denominator
theology' at the centre of the Church of England. There is
no plot. It is simply the fruit of synodical government, its
proportional representation and its voting systems (together
with the devil and human sinfulness).

Issues in human sexuality

Sadly, the Church is not only adrift in terms of doctrine: it is
also morally adrift. The House of Bishops collegially (for so
they now work) must bear much of the blame and, not least,
in the matter of homosexual behaviour.

There was a significant occasion, a little later than the
debate over *The Nature of Christian Belief*, that revealed

the drift (and weakness) of the late twentieth-century episcopate in the Church of England.

On 11 November 1987 in the General Synod I moved a
modest amendment for some sort of church discipline in the
context of a debate on homosexual relations. This would only
affect the clergy; nor was it unfairly isolating homosexual
behaviour: it was merely asking for 'appropriate discipline'
– appropriateness being left to the pastoral discretion of the
bishop concerned. It said this:

> if a bishop, priest or deacon is to be a 'wholesome
> example and pattern to the flock of Christ' (Canon C4)
> appropriate discipline among the clergy should be exer-
> cised in cases of sexual immorality.

It failed. This was because of the voting of the House of
Clergy and the House of Bishops, with the bishops being
most opposed to it. They rejected it by 14 votes to 5. The
laity, however, supported this amendment by 136 to 84. The
press then, not unreasonably, attacked the bishops for moral
cowardice.

So with this track record it was not surprising that in
1991 the bishops took tentative steps and virtually validated
homosexual sex for lay people. This was in their report *Issues
in Human Sexuality*. Parts of the report are quite good, but
when they came to the key issue of homosexuality this is what
they said:

> it is . . . only right that there should be an open and wel-
> coming place in the Christian community both for those
> homophiles who follow the way of abstinence, giving
> themselves to friendship for many rather than intimacy
> with one, and *also for those who are conscientiously con-
> vinced that a faithful, sexually active relationship with one
> person, aimed at helping both partners to grow in disciple-
> ship, is the way of life God wills for them* [italics mine].

The bishops have excluded, at present, clergy from this openness to homosexual sex.

Evangelical bishops who, no doubt, were at Keele have agreed to this report as a corporate document. There was not a single word of dissent. The new Bishop of Durham, who claims personally to have repented of former criminal homosexual activity, has agreed to this report and today appeals to it.

Conscience

In the report the bishops refer to the traditional teaching on the 'conscience':

> Christian tradition . . . contains an emphasis on respect for free conscientious judgement where the individual has seriously weighed the issues involved.

Their argument for accepting (lay) homosexual sex hinges round their commitment to the 'conscience'. But what the bishops are doing is this: they are employing the general conclusion of the traditional, medieval teaching about conscience, and respect for it; however, they are ignoring the detailed qualifications that must go along with that conclusion.

The bishops should have spelt out some of the essentials of this traditional teaching. These include the following. First, the paradigm case involving conscience is the duty to obey God rather than man as in Acts 5:29. Secondly, there must be a distinction made between a good conscience and one that is in error. And, thirdly, there must be a further distinction made between 'vincible' and 'invincible' error – error that can, and cannot, be corrected. A conscience in 'invincible' error might today be called 'pathological' and so is more excusable. A conscience in 'vincible' error is morally guilty because it could and should have seen the truth. A conscience of a rational person that contradicts the clear teaching of the Bible is always in 'vincible' error and so guilty.

Now the case the bishops have in mind, if it is ruthlessly spelt out (as it must be in moral argument), is of a 'conscience conviction' that permits a person to engage in habitual acts of anal intercourse or other same-sex genital activity on the grounds that this is not promiscuous; it is 'aimed at helping both partners to grow in discipleship'; and it 'is the way of life God wills for them'. And because this comes from their 'conscience' they are to have a welcome place in the Church and 'we stand alongside them in the fellowship of the Church'. But this case, of course, bears no relationship whatsoever to the paradigm; it certainly is not the result of a good conscience; and it most certainly is a case of 'vincible' not 'invincible' error, for it transgresses a clear biblical and church mandate. As the bishops themselves admit:

> there is . . . in Scripture an evolving convergence . . .
> Sexual activity of any kind outside marriage comes to
> be seen as sinful, and homosexual practice as especially
> dishonourable.

According to tradition such a 'conscientious conviction' of a 'vincible' error should *not* be encouraged or followed. It is worth noting that there is a further distinction to be made within 'vincible' error – between what such a conscience *permits* and what it *forbids*. As in the bishops' case, where a 'vincibly' errant conscience is permissive, it most certainly must not be followed. However, the traditional argument was that where it forbids something, it should be followed (i.e. in abstinence) until the error was discovered. This was, so it was said, because conscience errs more often through being too liberal than through being too strict. (It is, of course, these progressive qualifications that throw this whole tradition into disrepute. Nevertheless the bishops are claiming the moral authority of this tradition: they need to know what they are claiming!)

To summarise, the bishops are seeming to validate homosexual sex. They do not do this through the clear teaching of the Bible; they do it through an appeal to the conclusions of a medieval tradition, the helpfulness of which may be questioned anyway. But I have tried to show that the bishops have not even been fair to this tradition, which if applied consistently can make some legitimate distinctions.

Drift

There has undoubtedly been a drift since Nottingham (the subsequent Conference) in 1977, if not since Keele itself in 1966. A number of the evangelical bishops that are now validating conscientious homosexual sex among the laity in 1977 signed up to the Nottingham Statement. But that statement implied no validation for homosexual sex at all; it indeed wanted there to be a 'welcoming place' for Christian homosexuals; but it was assumed this was only for those Christian homosexuals 'who follow the way of abstinence' or try to. In those days evangelicals never dreamt it was necessary to say otherwise. So the resolution simply said:

> There should be a full welcoming place in the Christian fellowship for the Christian homosexual. Nevertheless, we believe homosexual intercourse to be contrary to God's law and not a true expression of human sexuality as he has given it.

At the beginning of 1995 many evangelical bishops were present at a London conference convened to promote evangelical unity. Prior to the meeting the Council of REFORM had written to all the episcopal participants asking them to affirm 'for the avoidance of doubt . . . that those clergy *and* laity who are "convinced that a faithful, sexually active relationship with one person (of the same sex), aimed at helping both partners to grow in discipleship, is the way of life God wills for them" are in grave error and are breaking God's law, whether they are conscientiously so convinced or not'. This was, of course, the wording from the bishops' report. Not one made that public affirmation.

Scribes and pharisees

The chairman of the conference, the Bishop of Chester, Michael Baughen, conspicuously only affirmed what the bishops' report had already affirmed. He however used the language of Nottingham 1977 that homosexual intercourse is contrary to 'God's law' rather than the report's 'God-given moral order'. But the problem is not a failure to assert God's law, ideal or moral order. The report is good on that. The problem comes from what the report then adds. This, as with the scribes and Pharisees, 'nullifies' the law of God. The scribes and Pharisees affirmed the law but their casuistry allowed them to defy it (Matthew 15:6). The bishops posit a dialectic between God's law and human freedom. And they remind us, in a concluding hint, that it is quite possible for 'love [to be] summoning the Church to rethink its existing perception of the truth'. That is why simple affirmations as the Bishop of Chester without denials made, in the world of modern bishops, is compatible with saying that homosexual genital acts, while wrong from the perspective of the Church, are right for a person who conscientiously thinks they are right.

This may shock some (sadly, I suspect, not all) of the evangelical bishops. But this is the logic of what they have together said and refused to distance themselves from. All this is no more than conventional moral relativism. At a popular level many ascribe to it in the wider world (and the Church) today. There may be absolutes and ideals. But they are relative to individual circumstances. Behaviours and beliefs can only be said to be 'right for me'.

The bishops in their report tell us that there is an 'historic tension in Christian ethical thinking between the God-given moral order and the freedom of the moral agent'. But that tension, they imply, allows for the creation of *new* ideals. They say:

> The ideal of chastity holds good for all Christians; and homophiles who do not renounce all physical sex relations must nevertheless be guided by some form of that ideal appropriate to them.

What is this if not a new ideal alongside and contradicting the old ideal?

Some bishops may delude themselves by saying that all they are proposing in the report is that when active homosexuals come into your church, you do not immediately eject them! But, of course, the text of the report says much more than that. Indeed if the bishops really meant only that, it would imply a proposal to eject all but a precisely defined class of homosexuals. You should therefore eject all promiscuous homosexuals who may visit your church and who do not have the hypocrisy to believe that their behaviour is the path of Christian discipleship. But, surely, these are people you ought to help towards salvation and wholeness.

The report is tragic evidence that the Church of England is morally adrift and in need of reform.

Social significance

But the Church is adrift not only doctrinally and morally; it is also adrift in terms of social significance. This is related to its numerical decline. The latest *Church Statistics* for 1994 indicate that not only are the stipendiary clergy showing a drop in numbers; but usual Sunday attendances – the key index in church growth terms – are also decreasing.[3] Only 2.3 per cent of the population are now in an Anglican place of worship in England on any given Sunday. The decline is small – 14,400 per year in terms of average Sunday attendance – but decline it is. A loss of social significance is serious as leading to an inability to communicate with those outside.

Furthermore the Anglican Communion worldwide is losing social significance. Currently there are 57.4 million Anglicans in the world. By the year 2000 the world population should have increased by 8 per cent. But it is estimated that Anglicans worldwide will only have increased by 3 per cent (*International Bulletin of Missionary Research*, January 1995). The encouraging Anglican growth in the two-thirds world is offset by decline in the first world.

Also the pull and the relevance of 'denominationalism' – of Anglicanism as such – is now receding. This further contributes to the diminishing of the social strength of Anglicanism. In *Congregational Studies: The Unexplored Territory*, J. P. Wind makes the observation from his research in the United States (where more work has been done than here on the sociology of denominations) that 'Denominations used to be primary supporters of congregational identity . . . they now find themselves filling new fiscal, regulatory and public policy roles.'[4] That is true of England as well, and the Church of England. The majority of people now choose their church not by any denominational label but by its performance – the quality of its ministry; its doctrinal position; the competence of its clergy; the preaching; the music; its earned reputation and its public visibility. The denomination now comes about tenth or eleventh on the list.

My *fourth* assumption is that the Church, to quote Hooker, has to be seen as a 'society and a society supernatural'. Therefore attention has to be paid to both organisational and theological issues at the same time. This is a wonderful recipe for misunderstanding. Many people will think you are concerned with structures when you are concerned with doctrine, and doctrine when you are concerned with structures.

Organisational requirements

My *fifth* assumption is that for any organisation (secular or religious) to function well four things are needed: an agreed agenda; competent leadership; enabling structures; and market (or client) sensitivity.

First, all have to be going in the same direction with an agreed agenda. The Church of England no longer has that. This is a trade-off from its current pluralism. The problems are obvious. You cannot easily have some people thinking that extramarital sex and homosexual intercourse are legitimate, in the same boat as others who vigorously think the opposite; or, to take an example relevant to prison service chaplains, you cannot easily have some people who want to accommodate paganism (including witchcraft) in the same boat as others who believe that is apostasy.

Secondly, competent leadership is vital. But many ordinands come out of existing Anglican theological colleges and courses ill-equipped for ministry in today's world. There is weakness in their preaching and application of the gospel of Christ and a weakness in parochial leadership skills.

Thirdly, enabling structures must be in place for institutional health. But there has now evolved a Diocesan and General Synod bureaucratic centralism since the advent of synodical government in 1970. This has resulted in passivity among the clergy and passivity among the laity in the congregations. Most interestingly, while the numbers of parochial clergy have been reduced the number of dignitaries has increased. In 1961 (when I was a student) there were 12,886 parochial clergy and 231 dignitaries. Thirty years later in 1991 there were 9,611 parochial clergy and 385 dignitaries. There has been a 25 per cent reduction in parochial clergy and a 66 per cent increase in dignitaries. We now have an Anglican centralism in the dioceses and at the General Synod that absorbs too large a proportion of diocesan budgets. Furthermore, key decisions are now being taken by diocesan officials and bureaucrats who have a vested interest in keeping the centre going.

Ivan Illich once spoke of professionals who 'need clients to survive' and cynically suggested that

> . . . they create and define problems, diseases and deficiencies which they, and they only, have the skills to put right. They disable their clients in order to enable them, creating thereby a spurious dependency and problems which need never have been invented.[5]

This is too near the reality of many 'diocesan centres' in the Church of England for comfort.

Reform

My *sixth* assumption is that reform in any organisation normally comes from the bottom or the edges. Canon Marriott said many years ago:

> History offers few examples of an institution which effects its own revival. In the majority of cases that is brought about by a minority movement within its borders. Christianity was itself such a movement, so was Franciscanism, so was Wesleyanism, so was Tractarianism.[6]

My *seventh* assumption is that attempts by evangelical Christians to reform the Church of England since the war have not succeeded. I have been party to those attempts. I believe it was right to have tried. But the result of evangelical 'entryism' following Keele in 1967 has been that evangelicals have had a larger and larger slice of the Anglican cake; but many of those evangelicals appear to have 'gone native' – not least those appointed to high office. They often seem to end up being as ineffective as those they seek to reform.

My *eighth* assumption relates to the quincentenary of the birth of William Tyndale (the day this paper was originally given). As one of the initiators of REFORM in the Church of England, I would like to think we were assuming, in a much humbler way, the vision of Tyndale. He reminds us of the need for a group like REFORM.

Tyndale

First, Tyndale was concerned for the fundamentals of the gospel, with the gospel of salvation by grace through faith in Christ being at its heart. The means to that salvation was a knowledge of the Bible, hence the need for translation. And the Bible was 'perspicuous'. Tyndale asserted that the Scriptures could be 'truly understood, after the plain places and general articles of the faith'. There was no great hermeneutical problem over the things that mattered. If your heart was right with God, you would understand the Bible. This was the message of his *Pathway into the Holy Scripture*.

Secondly, Tyndale knew that the situation was desperate. It was not just that the Church was at sea; it was nearing, or on, the rocks. Something had to be done. This distinguished Tyndale from, say, Erasmus. Erasmus saw the problems but he would not act. Erasmus was the first one to talk of the desirability of 'the husbandman singing parts [of the Bible] at his plough'. But in a candid letter to Ricard Pace he wrote these words: 'I follow the Pope and the Emperor when they decide well, because it is pious to do so; I bear their bad decisions, because it is safe to do so.'

This is the challenge to us today – not just to analyse and complain but to act and not to remain 'safe' – to cap quotas; to plan alternative training; and to evangelise across parochial boundaries if necessary.

Man of action

When Bishop Tunstall (in whose chapel this paper was originally given) refused Tyndale his patronage and a licence, Tyndale went ahead with his translation work all the same. But Tyndale was not a hot-head. He realised that secondary matters had to be ignored. Writing to his friend John Frith about handling a matter of secondary importance he told him to 'laugh and let it pass, and refer the thing to other men, and stick you stiffly and stubbornly in earnest and necessary things'. Tyndale, though, took action when necessary. His great life's work, the English Bible, is a testimony to his being a man of courage and his passion for the gospel of Christ.

And he could call a spade a spade. He called Wolsey, 'Caiaphas the Cardinal'; Bishop Tunstall 'that Saturn, the imaginer of all mischief' and 'a ducking hypocrite, made to dissemble', while other bishops were 'blind buzzards and shameless hypocrites'. They were.

Tyndale was no 'hireling' – a clergyman who feeds the sheep but when the wolf comes takes cover because he is basically in the job for himself. No, Tyndale faced the wolf and cleverly defeated the wolf. He was as wise as a serpent; or, to change the metaphor, he played his cards well. But praise God, just one year after his martyrdom in 1536, an English Bible received a royal licence in 1537. Soon there was an English Bible in every church in the land. Tyndale, indeed, was a great reformer.

How we need reformers to follow in his footsteps today! And REFORM, in a small way, is seeking to do just that. It is a network of Anglican individuals and parishes committed on the one hand to the biblical gospel of Jesus Christ and on the other hand to principled action to evangelise the nation and to make the parishes of this land once again the heart of the Church of England.

3

The case against REFORM

Peter Baron

Peter Baron is Curate of St Peter's, Monkseaton, in the Diocese of Newcastle. For much of 1994 he waged almost single-handedly a campaign against REFORM in the pages of *Church Times*.

Three evangelicals, an Arminian, a Calvinist and a charismatic died, and to their consternation found themselves in hell. The Arminian, believing as they do in personal responsibility, complained: 'I'm here because I made the wrong choice somewhere.' The Calvinist moaned to himself: 'I'm here because I've been predestined to destruction before the foundation of the world.' The charismatic smiled and raised his hands and said simply: 'I'm not here.' Or perhaps: 'I'm not here, I'm in Toronto!'

That story illustrates how evangelicalism has always been divided by doctrine and church practices. It is easy to caricature. Broadly, an evangelical may be defined as someone who elevates the authority of Scripture, who believes in the conversion of individuals, and exalts the cross in doctrine and spirituality: I will leave the subtlety of definition there. As a conservative evangelical (one who seeks to conserve orthodox doctrine), I have spent most of the last eighteen years in large evangelical churches. I was faithfully pastored by long-suffering members of REFORM, I owe them much, and I find myself now stepping back and disagreeing with them, I hope 'in love'. How can this be?

Part of it may be due to differences in personality, and part of it to the problems evangelicals have in admitting that they are as culturally conditioned as the liberal or the charismatic. Evangelicals need to admit that they operate in tight interpretative communities, and that these can easily place boundaries on their exploration of Scripture and can colour their perception of the wider Church. In other words, evangelicalism is much more a cultural phenomenon than we realise: our commitment to the 'things which cannot be shaken' should not prevent us analysing critically the relationship between the ideas of our time and the beliefs and practices of today's evangelicals.

Where does REFORM locate on the spectrum of evangelicalism? Some see REFORM as the last attempt by Puritanism to influence the Church of England. I see it much more as a sociological phenomenon: about sub-groups and power and perception. REFORM, if it represents a death-throe, represents the last rites of the male, Western, Enlightenment and privileged sub-culture of evangelicalism.

REFORM was established in February 1993. A council of twenty-two leaders pledged themselves to 'a network of fellowship, bringing in individuals and parishes, through which we can pray together and support one another'. It was no coincidence that the foundation of REFORM coincided closely with the vote for the ordination of women to the priesthood (November 1992), even though many REFORM leaders maintained at the time that its members took different views on this issue. Despite calls by John Moore,[1] head of CPAS, to drop this from their agenda, opposition to women's headship remained one of the planks of the covenant which all parish clergy were invited to sign in the summer of 1994. 'Our understanding of God's way of life for his people', read a key clause of the covenant, 'includes the unique value of women's ministry in the local congregation but also the divine order of male headship, which makes the headship of women as priests in charge, incumbents, dignitaries and bishops inappropriate'.

The impetus of the women's issue in the founding of RE-FORM should not be underestimated. It explains their call for their own flying bishop in February 1994. But REFORM is far from a single-issue pressure group. There is also a deep-rooted unease with the way diocesan finances and deployment are handled, and a feeling that 'liberals' were disproportionately elevated in the Church hierarchy under Robert Runcie. This 'liberalism', they argue, has also infected the evangelical bishops, who are forced to act and speak together on doctrine and ethics even when the conclusions seem to go against an orthodox biblical view. They cite the 1986 bishops' report, *The Nature of Christian Belief* as an example.[2] At the heart of this debate about evangelicalism there are two issues which I will attempt to address: the issue of evangelicals' approach to the interpretation of Scripture, and their view of the nature of the Church.

Here I pursue two criticisms of REFORM which I believe are interconnected. The first is that their approach to biblical interpretation is stuck in a reaction to modernity, and as such is much more culturally determined than REFORM leaders will admit. I hope to show how it follows that REFORM invokes a male, Western and Enlightenment approach to biblical interpretation. The second, related issue, is that their idea of the Church elevates the local parish in a way that contradicts the 39 Articles and such ideas of the Church as we find in Scripture. It feels like a justification for a long-standing practice in their churches, which have often operated as eclectic congregations a little like cathedrals,[3] with their own quasi-bishops exercising tight authority over their flocks.

This question remains: does their idea of the Church colour their interpretation of Scripture? Or does their exegesis of Scripture affect their idea of the Church? Or is the relationship in some way *reciprocal*?

The hermeneutics of modernity

At the risk of being guilty of the caricatures I warned about at the beginning, I want to contrast two types of evangelical. The first was born out of the Keele Congress of 1967. 'The place of Keele', argues David Bebbington in his scholarly account of evangelicalism in the last two hundred years,[4] 'in the development of evangelicalism in the Church of England has been compared to that of the Second Vatican Council in the Roman Catholic Church.' At Keele, evangelicals committed themselves to be involved in the remodelling of the Church of England, in its liturgy and church government. More significantly for my argument here, evangelicals admitted that they had occupied a ghetto, and that the ghetto was self-inflicted.

'A closed mind', argued one speaker, 'is a denial of the Holy Spirit . . . and evangelicals in the twentieth century have not been conspicuous for open-mindedness.'[5] The final Statement showed remarkable humility when it declared: 'We, who know ourselves to be prone to error and infected by sin, wish to join in conversation with others similarly affected, yet who profess to know God's grace . . . We recognise that in dialogue we may hope to learn truths held by others to which we have hitherto been blind.'[6]

Keele therefore established the idea of the open evangelical. An open evangelical is not the same thing as a 'liberal' (whatever that word means!). 'Open' means open to listen, discuss and develop, to take the risk that in listening to someone of a different view, even a 'liberal' view, one's own views may change or be modified. It does not mean an abandonment of traditional evangelical beliefs about the atonement and scriptural authority.

As John Stott put it at the Nottingham Congress of 1977, evangelicals are gospel people and Bible people. This means they have an *a priori* commitment to Scripture, but 'nothing is sacrosanct to the radical conservative Christian except Scripture itself.' Unfortunately, the debate that began at Nottingham about biblical interpretation, and made more pressing by the foundation of REFORM, has not really taken off. Evangelicals are too ready to say 'I do not understand your interpretation', when they really mean 'I do not understand the different approaches to interpretation demanded by different texts.'

The open evangelicalism of Keele can be contrasted with the closed evangelicalism of the ghetto before Keele. The theology of the Church before 1967 was that of the remnant: the true Church against the Church of England, or even the true believer against his unconverted congregation. This view, which seems to be resurrected by REFORM, is a product of the experience of theological education and the practice of evangelical churches in the 1950s and 1960s. There is a growing divide between the present leaders of REFORM, and those evangelicals dispersed throughout non-evangelical churches. This latter group have to be open, because they are dispersed. But this reality on the ground means that their theology of the Church cannot be the theology of the remnant. Instead it has to be a theology of dispersion and involvement.

Evangelicalism that is stuck in a reaction to modernity (henceforth referred to as 'closed evangelicalism') tends to have three features: *dualism*, in the distinction between subject and object and text and reader; a belief in *perspicuity* or clarity of Scripture, which tends to be overstated and inconsistently applied; and a tendency to let the system of thought and *dogma* control exegesis, rather than be truly liberated by the text.

Dualistic

The modern world of the Enlightenment ('modernity')[7] came to believe that empiricism, the objective proof of things in the external world, replaced other dimensions of reality. By the twentieth century metaphysics had died out in universities, to such an extent that God was not a word that was allowable because the God-concept had no truth claims verifiable within it. God had become separated from creation just as surely as the objective world had become separated from the subjective and fact from opinion.

Closed evangelicalism derives its own subject/object distinction from the Reformation. Article XIX of the 39 Articles emphasises the pure word preached: there is something pure about Scripture. The famous catchphrase of the Reformation goes: Christ rules and reigns by the sceptre of his word.

Yet the Word had become somehow objectified.[8] It had become given, the same for everyone, entirely definite, standing out in clear contrast to the human and subjective. We had the seeds here of that strange word 'infallibility' and its fundamentalist brother 'inerrancy', which have begged questions of evangelicals in the past.

Luther actually went further than this: 'nor am I speaking of the written word but rather the spoken gospel', or gospel preached. That sentence neatly dodges the entire problem of interpretation, how does the preacher step back from himself and decide which interpretation is correct, and how does he or she handle disagreements in interpretation?

The Reformation encountered this problem early on and the answer they gave was very clerical: only the called, tested and authorised minister was able to interpret. Of course, in principle, Reformers believed in the priesthood of all believers. In principle, as Lambert, a former monk, argued in 1526, it is the 'community of believers which can faithfully interpret the word of God'. But when the pattern of church government he drew for Prince Philip of Hesse did not conform with Luther's ideas, Luther had it suppressed. An interpretation was already being enforced from above. Notice, then, how an idea of the Church collapsed into hermeneutics, a way of interpreting the Bible, and dilemmas of authority become excuses for authoritarianism.

As Paul Avis[9] argued, the two distinguishing marks of the true Church *either* die the death of a thousand qualifications *or* make Protestant and Catholic ideas of the Church indistinguishable. Interpretations of these words 'pure gospel' were as varied as evangelical opinions on slavery in the eighteenth or social reform in the nineteenth century. Bullinger, successor to Zwingli, came nearest to exposing the real problem when he wrote: 'we embrace and retain the true sense'. But how do we arrive at the true or literal sense? This is a question of interpretation or hermeneutics.

Cranmer, interestingly, chose a form of reformed catholicism in regard to the relation between Scripture and its

interpretation. The early Church fathers became the defining
authoritative period for interpretation. Interpretation cannot
be separated from community, nor community from tradition.
It just depends which community and which portion of tradition is chosen. The more closed the community, the more
rigid and non-negotiable will be the interpretation.

Closed evangelicalism tends to argue for 'timeless truths'
unambiguously derived. It can only do so by retaining a
tight control over interpretation. Its congregations will not
be invited to find new readings. Testimonies will be very uniform. There is no place for disagreement or multiple readings
of Bible texts. Language will be regimented and imagination stunted. All this is a reaction to the onslaught on the
Bible posed by liberal critics and the quest for the historical Jesus. The opposite to myth in modernity is historical
truth, and historical means 'out there in unambiguous space
and time'. The place of reader, interpreter and community
is neatly sidestepped: the leader becomes all, passing on a
timeless baton in a gospel relay race.

Closed evangelicalism, then, is a return to the thinking
which predates Keele.

The perspicuity of Scripture

Closed evangelicalism often seems blind to its own pre-
selection of texts. Evangelicals believe that the Old Testament
is as authoritative as the New. Yet some parts are more
functionally authoritative than others. As Thomas Erskine
pointed out two hundred years ago: 'the most zealous
defenders of the verbal inspiration of the Bible admit that
there are parts of it of less importance than others. This is a
great admission, because another is involved in it, namely that
we ourselves must be judges of the comparative importance
of different parts.' Is the 'we' here, we the community, or
the royal (authoritarian) we?

Much the same could be said of the appeal to the perspicuity of Scripture, a belief that REFORM argues we have lost. Here REFORM goes beyond what the Reformers would argue. Where Scripture is clear about the central message, faith in Christ crucified, it is much less clear about the subtleties of doctrine (the doctrine of substitutionary atonement, for instance, is derived by intricate argument and is often read back into texts such as Mark 10:45), and is highly contentious on secondary issues such as the ordination of women.

Closed evangelicalism tends to equate a belief in the rightness of women's headship with a rejection of Paul's apostolic authority. Again, this misses the point. It is the interpretation of the whole of Paul in the light of the whole of Scripture that is at issue. Many evangelicals, whilst exalting the authority of Scripture, do not find it clear that Paul opposed women's headship even if he said to one church in a pastoral letter: 'I do not allow women to have authority over a man' (1 Timothy 2:12). Even if he did, it must apply as much in politics as to the Church as to the police force as to every walk of life: somehow people manage to argue, 'Of course I'm voting for Mrs Thatcher as Prime Minister, she's the best man for the job, but no way a woman can head up my church!'

As John Stott argues,[10] 'the inspired text is also the partially closed text'. Because it is partially closed, we need preachers. Scripture comments of Paul 'there are many things hard to understand' (2 Peter 3:16). Exposition is important. It isn't easy or even clear-cut: even if the Bible was dictated by the Holy Spirit, its meaning can only emerge by an ongoing conversation between the text, each other, and all the books I have time to read. The Bible was written by community, to be read in community and it is community that teaches us how to read it, a function REFORM churches illustrate very well, even if their communities are relatively closed.

This closed evangelicalism also has difficulty with the many meanings inherent in Scripture. This, too, is its legacy from modernity. For liberals used the multivalence of Scripture to destroy the doctrinal core of faith. Not surprisingly, evangelicals reacted by arguing for one clear meaning. Such a reaction

resulted in the Chicago Statement of 1978 and the debates
between the inerrantists and the supremacists in the 1920s.

The Chicago Statement repeats modernity's subject/object
distinction, and the Enlightenment confidence in 'facts'. It also
shows exactly how, driven by the desire to create and defend
a watertight system, one can easily descend into philosophi-
cal absurdity. Article VI of the Chicago Statement on Biblical
Interpretation of 1982 states: 'We affirm that the Bible
expresses God's truth in propositional statements, and we
declare that biblical truth is both objective and absolute. We
further affirm that a statement is true if it represents matters as
they really are, but it is an error if it misrepresents the facts.'

There is little understanding here of the role of parable,
story or poetry in biblical narrative, nor how meaning exists
at different levels within propositions, nor how metaphor
works, nor how the reader creates meaning out of a context which includes, to quote Wittgenstein, his or her own
language-games and skills acquired in playing them. Article
XXII of the Chicago Statement goes on to 'affirm that Genesis
1–11 is factual'. Would the author of Genesis have held this
modernist view of 'fact'? Can a document not be truthful
without having to be 'factual'?

The leaders of REFORM erroneously appear to believe that
their culturally-conditioned view of fact and their philosophi-
cally untenable assertion of clarity are the only views possible
for those who hold to the firm foundations of the faith.

Closed evangelicalism loves the Chicago Statement. It is
stuck in modernity.

Dogmatic

Closed evangelicalism is a creation of systematic theology,
not story. It is logically neat and tied up. There are few
frizzy edges or partial answers, what Tom Wright calls 'the
scriptural basis for residual untidiness'.[11]

I am not sure whether evangelicalism creates its systematic

theology from its exegesis, as sometimes claimed, or vice versa. I suspect we hand on our spectacles within tight sub-cultures, and then become seriously worried when someone, or something, subverts it, as the creation of women presbyters did.

Again we have come full circle. For it is only the place of Scriptures lived in community which stops interpretation hardening into an over-confident dogmatism.[12] If this sounds too catholic, it is because the Catholic Church is correct on this. Sound reasoning must be applied. Reason, tradition and revelation cannot be prised apart in the ways some evangelicals imply, nor should the place of encounter and experience be dismissed, as the present wave of charismatic revival (sometimes called the Toronto blessing) illustrates.

Here the open evangelical follows, as in some ways in its ecclesiology, the example of Hooker. Hooker recognised that the mere Scriptures are not sufficient. We need the authority of the Church and the preacher to induce us to consider them favourably. And we need reason to apply the Scriptures as true revelation (evangelicals proceed on the assumption, *a priori*, that the Bible is true revelation). Reason also teaches us those moral duties not given in Scripture (to take out sensible insurance when borrowing a friend's car), and allows us to distinguish between the clear and the unclear, and between those parts we follow to the letter, and those parts, such as Joshua's love of ethnic cleansing, we would tend to eschew.

We need to replace an outdated and redundant hermeneutic with a liberating, engaged hermeneutic for a postmodern world.[13] REFORM, in failing to understand how different interpretations can come from the same text, and how different texts require different rules of interpretation, proves that the great call of the Nottingham Congress of 1977, to engage with hermeneutics, has not been heeded.[14]

An Anglican evangelical idea of the Church

In REFORM's agenda we find three questions emerging which are very much questions that emerged during the Reformation of the sixteenth century, but which the different Reformers continued to grapple with: 1. Where is the Church? 2. What are the marks of the true Church (*notae ecclesiae*)? 3. What is the boundary of the true Church?

Question 1: Where is the Church? The visible and invisible dimensions

Luther believed that the true Church was 'not a physical assembly, but an assembly of hearts in one faith'. The Church thus became *invisible*: 'the church is a deep, hidden thing which one may neither see nor perceive but must grasp only by faith through baptism, sacrament and word'.

Hooker[15] warned us of the problems that result from a failure to distinguish between the visible and invisible Church. But the more radical Reformers proved that, when the principle of invisibility was pursued to its logical conclusion, it became a demand for purity and entailed a denial of the validity of any visible manifestation.[16] REFORM appears, by its practice and some of its published documents, to be pursuing this idea of the pure Church.

In distancing himself from the radicals, Luther was forced to embrace a doctrine of the visible Church as the divinely ordained means of grace.[17] This had two effects. It paved the way for the clerical dominance that soon choked the Reformation. And it meant that Augustine's view of the Church as the inclusive organisation of saints and sinners, wheat and tares, which Luther and the English Reformers tended to favour and which is enshrined in Article XXVI ('in the visible church the evil be ever mingled with the good'), came up against the practical necessity to condemn the pope, and the Catholic doctrine of visible historical continuity. It was this necessity that led the Reformers to identify the marks of the true Church.

How does this debate affect today's? The temptation within evangelicalism is to define the true Church as invisible, but then to argue that the moral life of the visible body should conform to it. Where it does not conform, REFORM argues, there is a need for pastoral discipline and on occasions, the withholding of money. The implication is that the true Church is invisible, but definable, and that the Anglican Church should therefore be reformed of its impurities. This appears to go against Luther, and Augustine and the English Reformers, and denies the essential paradox of Paul that they found so compelling: that he never declared the immoral Corinthians or backsliding Galatians as apostate – he never, in other words, allowed their visible impurities to lead him to doubt their invisible status.[18]

Question 2: What are the marks of the true Church?

Article XIX of the 39 Articles mentions two marks of the visible Church: the pure Word of God preached and the sacraments duly administered. The wording follows almost exactly the Augsburg Confession of 1530.[19] It represents a different emphasis from the thirteen articles of 1538, discovered in some papers belonging to Archbishop Cranmer, which reads 'the visible church is recognised by the profession of the gospel and the communion in the sacraments'.

Oliver O'Donovan[20] has convincingly shown how Cranmer opted out of the three-part relationship implied by the thirteen articles. The three points of the triangle comprise the *invisible* Church, which Article XIX fails to mention, and the particular and universal aspects of the visible Church. In the thirteen articles, the particular is represented by the word *profession*, and the universal aspect of the visible Church by the word *communion*, which implies something close to Hooker's idea of a sacramental fellowship united through time and across scattered space.

There are two errors we can fall into, therefore, in making the distinction between invisible and visible. One is to make the invisible a standard of purity and a reason to purify the Church visible. The second is to deny the catholic visible nature of the Church and confine it to one congregation (*ecclesia*). Intriguingly, Griffith Thomas, who produced an evangelical commentary on the 39 Articles, avoids this error. He divides the dimensions of the Church into three: local, general and universal,[21] where general 'is the aggregate of Christians in various places at one time (1 Cor. 10:32; 12:28)' and universal includes 'all Christians past, present and future (Eph. 1:22; 3:10)'.

Question 3: Where is the boundary of the true Church?

Luther's boundary of the Church was fuzzy, in contrast with REFORM's. Was it to be defined sacramentally? In which case the presbyter is the boundary policeman, denying or assenting to baptism, permitting or not permitting people to be accepted at the Lord's Table or as a 'true Christian'. Or could a boundary be defined by the centre (the pure Word preached that calls the Church into being)[22]?

Heirs to the Reformation tended to go two ways. Some drew in the boundary. Melanchthon, for example, progressively added discipline to his list of marks of the Church. By 1555 he came out with his strongest statement, the need for 'punishment through the ban'. Bucer wrote: Where there is no discipline and excommunication there is no Church. The Anabaptists, who were formed in 1521, the same year Luther was put under papal excommunication, tried to form a pure community not unlike the Essenes. Paradoxically they soon found a struggle between inspired and elected leaders, whereas Bucer and Melanchthon's ecclesiology simply became more and more clerical: it required the policemen to police.

The English Reformers generally took a more pragmatic

line. Hooker relaxed the boundary and produced an extensive ecclesiology. They were startled to find the charity Paul extended to the Corinthians and Galatians. Were papists still Christians? Hooker argued yes! What about our fathers in Christ? Anyone who professed 'one Lord, one faith, one baptism' argued Hooker. Yet we all need our pictures, models, interpretative keys. 'A picture,' said Wittgenstein, 'held me captive. I could not get outside it.' What is to be our picture of the Church? Evangelicals tend, in arguing about the Church, to take Pauline ones. I will start with Paul but then suggest two other sources for these pictures of the Church.

Paul uses a variety of metaphors: body, family,[23] tree. Consider the body metaphor of 1 Corinthians 12 or Ephesians 4:16. We could read this metaphor two ways, each way dialectically opposed. We could, as some Reformers did, take it as an argument for purity: the body represents Christ so expel the immoral brother![24]

But there's another way of reading Paul: the body is organic, and so still *developing*; it includes all kinds (weak and strong), so is *comprehensive* and no part is either indispensable or useless, which means we are *interdependent*.

The gospels produce a different picture which corresponds in some ways to a centre-circumference model.[25] At the centre is Jesus, then the three (Peter, James and John), then the other Apostles, then the disciples (men and women), then the crowd. Those nearest Jesus often seem the furthest away, and those beyond the pale are suddenly propelled into the centre, and like Bartimaeus, follow full of faith on the way. The boundary itself is very muzzy, so much so that those who liked nice distinctions couldn't face this radical who ate with tax gatherers and sinners and, God forbid, women. When the disciples tried to act like boundary policemen, as with the little children, Jesus became angry with them: it was as though there might be concentric circles, but no limit to the number of them and no man-made judgment as to who had crossed over.

The pictures in the Old Testament are summed up by various words: *qahal* (assembly in the desert, hence specific); *goi* (nation, hence widespread, corporate); *leom* (people, hence with common identity); *ir* (city, hence governed, as in Isaiah 1:21); *matteh, shebet* (tribe, hence travelling); *ets* (a vine tree, hence with branches). It was often dispersed, sometimes gathered, and, crucially, usually failing God and fallible. Of course, the New Testament picks up these ideas, for instance, in 1 Peter, possibly a baptismal document: 'you are a royal priesthood, a holy nation. God's own people'. The 'you' to which Peter refers were dispersed from Babylon to Northern Turkey, hardly a congregation in the sense REFORM seem frequently to argue, specific to one place. Even in the New Testament a theology of dispersion can be seen developing.

Indeed, biblically the Church does prove to have those three dimensions: invisible (a relationship with Christ and the assembly of saints in heaven); visible (a catholic dispersed family united by a communion of his body and blood, by common creeds and a common baptism); and visible local gathering, the outcrop of rock representing the one Church catholic.

To sum up, I would argue that evangelicals, particularly those who have joined REFORM, need to rediscover these three very Anglican marks of the Church in Scripture:

1. The Church *inclusive*: a social concept, a people of the open doors and listening ears, slow to judge, quick to listen and loath to purify.

2. The Church *comprehensive*: as doctrinally pluriform as the New Testament churches, but with one invisible Christological core.

3. The Church *fallible*. A people who confess weakness, who eschew modern power plays, who incarnate sin-redemption-resurrection. A place people outside can identify with but one that offers not just the hope, but the practice of transformation and of genuine forgiveness, where I can disagree and still call you brother or sister.

Has Keele failed?

The Keele Congress gave evangelicals the confidence and encouragement to open themselves to different theological traditions (including the liberal tradition). It is no contradiction to be described as an 'open conservative' evangelical. John Stott's leadership gave evangelicals that confidence, which was ably backed up by the writings of evangelical academics.

Today there are many more academics who are identifiably evangelical.[26] Much of their writing is prophetic. REFORM appears to disparage the lead they are taking, believing that to engage with new approaches to literary criticism and approaches to biblical interpretation is to sell out to the old enemy, 'liberalism'. The argument presented here is that REFORM itself, in taking this approach to Scripture, is betraying its own cultural roots in a reaction to modernity. This approach is outdated and inappropriate to the postmodern world. Not only will REFORM, if it gathers momentum, split evangelicals in the Church. It will also ensure that evangelicals who follow their lead repudiate Keele and Nottingham, reoccupy the ghetto, and group in eclectic churches whose walls become ever more rigid and whose contribution to the mission of England becomes ever more irrelevant. The future lies, not here, but in the dispersion of evangelicals in non-evangelical churches who are poised to answer the call of the Lambeth Conference of 1988 to make our national Church truly evangelical: a gospel people and a Bible people.

Evangelicals need urgently to be self-critical, in order to earn the authority to criticise the wider Church. Many of REFORM's criticisms of church structures may be valid, but if they are to be listened to, evangelicals must give up their claim to a non-negotiable certainty and to the rightness of their position and listen, not just to their own community, but also to the wider community of the Church and to the Church in history. When a member of REFORM's council circulated the House of Bishops listing their sins and calling them to repent, he demonstrated a lack of under-standing of episcopacy as well as an arrogance born of an over-confident approach to Scripture. To have a true con-versation, as Lesslie Newbigin has observed, involves a risk of conversion to the other person's viewpoint.[27]

REFORM themselves illustrate how tradition becomes normative: I have tried to show how I disagree with their interpretation of the Reformation ideas of the Church. These do not adequately consider the influence of Augustine on the Anglican Reformers (and indeed on Luther). I suspect it is their idea of the Church as the local congregation which con-trols their reading of Scripture,[28] and so blinds them to the biblical pictures of the Church *visible* and *universal*.

But it could be the other way round: that their exegesis defines their idea of the Church. For if, as I've argued, their interpretation is stuck in a reaction to modernity, it is capable of producing readings of text which other evangelicals will continue to brand unbiblical.

PART THREE

Keele Evangelicals on REFORM

4

Paying for ministry

Michael Turnbull

Michael Turnbull is the new evangelical Bishop of Durham. As Chairman of the Turnbull Commission he also has responsibility for the reform of the central organisation of the Church.

I don't think I would be telling tales out of school if I said that the title for this chapter had changed from 'An Option for the Poor' to 'Paying for Ministry'. However, I once heard a story about William Temple in his greats finals in Oxford. He was asked to write four essays out of a choice of ten subjects. He, in fact, wrote one essay covering all ten subjects and got a first! Well, I am not in that bracket. I will attempt to address briefly both the titles given to me. After all, clergy could be regarded as the poor and much of the Church Commissioners' work could be regarded as an option for them, and indeed for other, more obvious, poor. Their contribution to clergy stipends is still significant and without that a diocese like Durham, one of the poorest in the Church of England, could not cope. But let's look first at the principles behind the Church Commissioners; how they get their money and what they do with it.

The Church Commissioners originate from the 1704 Royal Charter of Queen Anne's Bounty, which expressed the commitment to provide for 'the augmentation of the maintenance of parsons, vicars, curates and ministers officiating in any church or chapel where the liturgy and rites of the Church of England are used and observed'. This is affirmed in the wording of the Ecclesiastical Commissioners' Act of 1840, which includes the words 'making additional provision for the cure of souls in parishes where such assistance is most required'.

Recently the Church Commissioners have put out a Mission

Statement of their own and part of this runs as follows: 'Our primary responsibility is to manage the investments entrusted to us to maximise our financial support for the ministry of the Church of England, particularly in areas of need and opportunity.'

Today, some of these ideals are fulfilled by selective allocations to dioceses for the purpose of clergy stipends. In 1986 the Commissioners produced a White Paper opting for targeting substantial new money on the needier dioceses. This enabled the needier dioceses to receive a much higher level of support. This 'weighting' took into account the historic resources of any individual diocese, the potential outcome and the level of unemployment in the area covered.

Of course, in the present climate, in order to bring their income and expenditure back into line, the Commissioners are now having to cut back on their stipend support for dioceses. This is being done in a way which seeks to sustain higher levels of allocation to the poorer dioceses for as long as possible. As it happens, Durham Diocese receives the highest selective allocation amounting to over £6,000 per annum per minister. At the other end of the scale, Peterborough Diocese receives only £500. In Durham Diocese the Church Commissioners pay about fifty per cent of the stipends bill, but this is the highest in the country by some distance. This hides, however, significant contributions from the Church Commissioners, towards the total cost of clergy. This includes pension provision, National Insurance contributions, and housing.

The Church Commissioners' contribution is rapidly decreasing because: a) investment income has not kept up with stipend increases; b) increasing pension demands from longer-living pensioners, and better pension packages; and c) the loss by the Church Commissioners of some invested capital value by property investment in the 1980s which has borne the brunt of the current economic recession.

The escalating shortfall has to be met by increased giving in parishes. The whole of the sum needed is calculated, collected and distributed by the diocese. The Diocese of Durham, for example, with its 280 paid clergy, has, therefore, deployment choices to make, which again will reflect the reality of an option for the poor.

It would be quite possible to put the paid clergy 'where the money is' and allow market forces to govern the distribution of clergy. But that would totally undermine the commitment of the Church of England of providing a place of worship and an accessible minister in every community – whether leafy suburb, country village, or inner city. The diocese has its own system of collecting funds from parishes and this is weighted so that more affluent parishes provide money to supplement the cost of ministry in poor areas. Therefore, in terms of its chief material assets – people and buildings – the Church of England could be said to be deployed with the poor in mind.

We are in a fast-changing situation as far as the Commissioners' contributions to ministry are concerned. Their investments are likely to play a diminishing role in the future funding of the whole Church. It is inevitable that the amounts available for allocation to the needier dioceses will be smaller than the Church has been used to over the last decade. They will, therefore, need to be targeted on a small number of dioceses, perhaps on a basis which specifically identifies mission areas and the most deprived parishes. But, properly focused, these allocations can still play a crucial role in keeping a Church presence in areas which other denominations have been forced, on economic grounds, to abandon. This will sustain the bias to the poor which historically has been a core purpose of the Commissioners.

Quite apart from stipend and pension provision for the clergy, there are a number of other activities which are worth mentioning which help to underline an option for the poor.

For instance, the Commissioners' policy helps with the regeneration of economically depressed areas. For some years the Commissioners have invested in a small number of small investment companies which were established to contribute towards the regeneration of such areas. One property investment held by the Commissioners has also contributed tangible and intangible benefits in this way and may be of particular interest to people in the North East. This is, of course, the MetroCentre in Gateshead, Tyneside, which was developed primarily for commercial purposes. Nevertheless it was sited in an enterprise zone and provided additional employment in the area. It now employs over 5,500 local people. The immediate neighbourhood of the MetroCentre has been improved by further development and local communities are less run-down than they were five years ago. There has also been a tourist spin-off for the whole region. The MetroCentre has its own full-time chaplain. There are community rooms available free of charge to charities and churches. A large amount of money is raised for charity.

Another area where the Church Commissioners work an option for the poor, is in the provision of affordable housing. The Commissioners cannot sell sites below their market value and are only able to promote sites which have not other development potential or which are part of a larger development where the affordable housing element constitutes planning gain. However, a number of sites have been sold for low-cost housing development where need is greatest though it has to be said that in the North, planning authorities seem more reluctant to designate sites solely for this purpose, even where a need for low-cost housing has been identified by those locally concerned.

Another example of this housing concern is in the traditional 'Octavia Hill' estates in London which provide over 1,600 units of good quality housing for those needing accommodation at modest rents. The system involves collecting rents, ordering repairs, selecting tenants and generally looking after their welfare. The lettings policy on these estates is a flexible one, geared in particular to meeting the needs of those who are not catered for by other housing bodies.

The Church Commissioners have also taken care that redundant churches and their sites are used for housing purposes. As at 31 December 1993, 105 redundant churches or redundant church sites had been sold to housing associations or local authorities for residential use.

The Commissioners have in the past given cash grants totalling £4 million to the Church Urban Fund which is committed to the regeneration of inner cities.

The Church Commissioners, in recent times, have had a bad press, and indeed it would be foolish to suppose that all was well within the financial structures of the Church. It would not be an exaggeration to say that we are living through a period of some crisis. But we are not alone amongst great institutions who, like us, are moving into new eras of financial provision, development and control. I am currently chairing, on behalf of the Archbishops, a commission that is looking at the central structures of the Church and that includes, of course, the Commissioners. I have no doubt that that will make proposals for fairly radical change. But all this should not detract from the fact that both the ideals of the Church Commissioners and the way in which they are operating today, in themselves provide a ministry which seeks to mirror, in financial terms, the kind of priority care which stems from the founder of the Church, Jesus Christ. I hope that in this brief chapter, I have been able to convey some of this concern and intent.

Postscript

The timing of this publication has caused me some embarrassment. I delivered the talk in Durham on 27 October 1994 and I write this postscript in December 1994. The book itself is likely to be read in the second half of 1995. In the intervening months the Archbishops' Commission, to which I referred in the concluding remarks, will have had many meetings, taken much evidence and presented its findings to the Archbishops.

Moreover, the purpose of the book has moved to being a documentation of evangelical perceptions of the Church of England and how they have changed since the Keele

Conference. Originally, as my text indicates, I was asked to speak on the Church Commissioners – An Option for the Poor.

However, there are links between the journeys we are making in terms of ecclesiology, structure and our use of resources. Within the Church of England we are asked to give expression to the body of Christ with episcopal leadership and synodical government. That makes for creativity rather than tidiness, for a sense of being on a journey together rather than having an inflexible set of structures. A dynamic Church is always in the process of formation and reformation. I believe that is consonant with a gospel which proclaims the kingdom of God, and with early Church teaching using the head and body metaphors.

But the historic position of the Church Commissioners sits awkwardly with that. Bishops are related only formally to the Commissioners, the Synod only obliquely. The Commissioners' direct accountability is to Parliament.

The concept of Bishop in Synod works well at diocesan level where a bishop naturally and regularly worships and consults with his people. They know their resources and the needs which define their distribution. At a national level it is more difficult to make the concept effective. Over forty diocesan bishops seek to work collegially but together they form only part of General Synod and, as a body, have no formal links with the Commissioners.

The money flows from the Commissioners' historic assets, defined as they are by legislation, to the dioceses. There, that money is joined by the dioceses' own resources, some historic and some live giving. From the dioceses some of the money flows to the General Synod for central services. The sources of money and the pools of money are thus confusing. Moreover, the distribution of money is often separated from an overall view of the policy of the Church.

And who makes that policy? The public perception may be that the Archbishop of Canterbury directs the Church but any holder of that office knows that he is caught between public expectation and a set of structures which at best often frustrate him by delay and at worst render him powerless.

Some believe that the General Synod controls policy. But is that realistic for a body which meets twice (and occasionally thrice) a year and which, by its method of election and mode of meeting, is sometimes accused of being unrepresentative of the majority of people in the parishes?

The Church Commissioners are able to control a good deal of policy, especially if the Church allows itself to be finance-led. The Commissioners decide, for instance, on the weighted distribution of money to the dioceses. They decide on allocation to bishops and cathedrals. They are significant arbiters in pastoral reorganisation and the use of church buildings. Some, but by no means all, Commissioners are elected by Synod and final accountability is to Parliament.

The bishops in their dioceses exert a strong influence on policy-making at local level and corporately at national level through the House of Bishops. But ultimately there is no guarantee that individual bishops will, in many areas of policy-making, follow the national line. Moreover the extent to which individual parishes (less still individual members) follow the policy of Bishop in Synod, is arbitrary. This is exemplified by some parishes, and often they are large, successful, evangelical parishes, taking finances into their own hands by 'capping'. While that is striking in financial terms it represents an attitude which has long been held that each parish sets its own policy regardless of the bishop and the diocese.

All this leads to a huge confusion of who sets what policy, which decisions are made where, and how different parts of the Church communicate with each other. We cannot hope for a tidy Church, even if it were desirable, but we can make progress towards reshaping the Church so that it can more readily say why it is there – nationally, regionally and locally – and who has responsibility for each expression of its mission.

The central structures have a crucial part to play in defining the mission policy of the church, in allocating resources (particularly of the ordained ministry and of historic financial

resources) and of enabling mission to take place at appropriate levels. Shaping the central structures to do that is at
the heart of the work of the Archbishops' Commission on
Organisation.

While important aspects of the mission of the Church of
England will take place at national level (through influence
on the political and cultural life of the nation) and at regional
level (by engaging in partnerships which can effect change), it
will always be at the local level that the cutting edge of the
gospel will be worked out most crucially. It is on the ability
of the local church to be effective in mission and holy in its
lifestyle and worship, that the future of the Church of England
will depend.

The challenge to the evangelical constituency is whether it
can accept that role for the local church and at the same time
grasp the opportunities which are presented by the catholicity
of the Church and the obligations and responsibilities which
that involves.

5

Training for ministry

John Pritchard

John Pritchard is Warden of Cranmer Hall, an evangelical
Church of England theological college.

When Anglicans are frustrated with the Church three of their
favourite strategies are to blame the System, the House of
Bishops or the theological colleges. Others must take up the
challenge for the first two institutions; my task is to reflect on
the future of theological education, and those marvellous and
maddening establishments, the colleges.

I want to look at three questions: What are the *problems*
we face?; What are the *principles* we need to employ for the
future?; and what are the *scenarios* which might emerge as we
look ahead?

What are the problems?

There's a temptation to say that I started with three and
managed to narrow them down to fifteen; but it is possible
to identify six in particular. The first is *financial*. It is obvious
but it must be named. The budget for the Advisory Board for
Ministry is approximately £6.5 million, or 50 per cent of the
total budget of the General Synod. It costs over £6,200 per
year to train someone at a college, twice as much as on
a theological course. That's big money in a Church where
finance is excruciatingly tight. The Church is looking for cuts
and theological education is a prime target.

The second problem is *methodological*. There is a process
of 'removal' which all theological colleges necessarily adopt,

whereby we take people out of their context, put them into a strange form of community and disgorge them two or three years later into yet another social and ecclesial setting. But listen to the practical theologians, or the liberation theologians, the feminist, black, political and local theologians, and they all tell us that theology is contextual: it relates to specific places in specific ways.

The theological question here is this: Where is theology properly done, and who does it belong to? Is it done chiefly in lecture rooms and libraries, and then applied (diluted to taste) in practical ministry somewhere else? Or is it done in the thick of battle, where ministry is being exercised with passion and precision, and a living, working theology is being forged? Which method would St Paul have recognised? Martin Luther said: 'A man becomes a theologian by living, dying and being damned; not by reading, thinking and speculating.'

The third problem is *practical*. There are some very basic questions here. Is the Church of England getting the clergy it needs? Can they preach, teach and manage resources? Can they create imaginative liturgy, pray, and lead others deeper into God? Do they understand society and culture and engage with it creatively and critically? The answer is often: 'Yes, but not very well.' The well-meaning but ineffective clergyman of popular television may indeed be a caricature, but he must have come from somewhere. Look around the average clergy Chapter meeting or Parochial Church Council and it's sometimes hard to remember that these are the successors of those early Christians who 'outlived, outthought and outdied' everyone around them.

Behind this of course, is a larger *ecclesiological* problem to do with the health of the Church for which theological education is preparing its women and men. There are continuing signs that the Church of England is unable to shake off its preoccupation with the agenda of the religious ghetto. Issues of disestablishment, the Church Commissioners' missing millions, lay presidency, homosexual clergy and others are simply not the concerns of most of the population, nor are they the signs of a vital and dynamic Church, confident in its Lord and its gospel. It would not be surprising if God were reluctant to raise up too many ordinands for a Church which is more concerned with moving the office furniture around than with renewing creation.

An extension of the ecclesiological problem is the question of the Church's *institutional* identity. The Church is currently sharing in the corporate 'dark night of the institution', whereby every sector of establishment life in society is coming under sharp criticism. Parliament, the monarchy, the police and legal profession, the education system and the health service – all the ancient or post-war landmarks are under scrutiny. The Church of England appears to be just another dinosaur gently collapsing towards oblivion through its inability to adapt to a changing climate. It hardly sounds like an ideal time to attract new recruits to keep the dinosaur standing.

And the sixth problem is *human*. The Church is at last sharing the cold blast of economic change and insecurity which has been society's typical experience for at least the last decade. No longer can Directors of Ordinands confidently offer a stipendiary post for life; clergy unemployment has become a real possibility. When a potential ordinand is weighing up the attractions of ministry, to add job insecurity to penury and stress makes the prospect less than compelling. Moreover, theological colleges are committed to a model of education which dislocates ordinands and their families twice in two or three years. The student gets the training; the spouse and children pay the price. Another human problem is that very many ordinands go through a time of depression in training – in both colleges and courses. One reason is that they are taking in so much more than they are giving out. In Christian terms it's an unbalanced diet. Receiving so much information and so many ideas, and processing so much personal change, while being forced to remain largely inactive in mission and ministry, creates spiritual indigestion.

These are some of the problems we face. They won't evaporate, but they must sharpen our thinking about the *principles* we will need to employ in a future strategy for theological education.

What are the principles?

First, theological education will have to be *missiological*, that is, directed outwards. For too long the Church of England has been managing decline with decorum. Damage limitation has been the strategy, and it's been hidden under the title 'pastoral re-organisation'. For generations we have operated on a chaplaincy model in our relation to society and its institutions, basing this approach on the supposition that British society is essentially Christian. This belief has now become so implausible that an honest reassessment of the Church's self-understanding is nothing short of vital. The call for a massive shift in the Church from a pastoral to a missionary paradigm has been made repeatedly, not least in the 1988 Lambeth Conference report. What has been slower to materialise is the necessary hard decision-making at every level of the Church's life in order to respond to the call. The question has to be put to every institution, committee, board, programme and appointment: Where is the mission dimension in this; in what way does this embody a response to a communicating and sending God?

The reality is that we do in fact have a gospel which is deeply needed not only by those who are attracted to religion, but by a whole world-order which is skidding off the tarmac. Theological education, therefore, must be confidently Christian, firing a new generation of clergy with a passion for the gospel of Christ as credible, necessary and effective. But with this proviso: it must be based on an understanding of God as One whose ways are inclusive and generous, not as One who seeks to disqualify people, and to draw tight boundaries around his chosen. The Decade of Evangelism can be confident without being triumphalistic, positive without being confrontational; and its inner character must be profligate love. The need is for clergy of quality who are capable of hard thinking and deep prayerfulness; people who understand that sacrifice is not an abstract concept but a lived experience of ministry; people who are not afraid of confrontation, love, vulnerability, passion, costly listening and waiting in the wilderness.

Second, theological education should be thoroughly *contextual*. The truth of the Christian revelation is not up for re-negotiation, but the way it engages with, and transforms, a situation is absolutely specific. We have to resist fiercely trying to take a universal gospel in universal ways to a supposedly universal people. God expresses himself uniquely in place and time. So in training, text and context have to be kept in constant dialogue: the hot steel of the gospel has to be poured into the changing moulds of society. Cranmer Hall, Durham, has an Urban Mission Centre in downtown Gateshead. Reading Romans 8 in a tower block in Gateshead is a significantly different experience from reading it in a student room in Durham. The text is rich enough to transform both, but it will do it very differently.

Moreover, this contextual dimension should mean that students see the central importance of embodying the truth they are exploring. Society has heard a lot of talking from the Church; it wants to see the action. People want to experience what the value of our high-sounding talk really is; to taste and see the committed edge of the gospel. This means rescuing students from the conspiracy of words which often bedevils theological education, and enabling them to experience and work with those who are embodying good practice, through whom 'the blind receive sight, the lame walk, the deaf hear, and the good news is preached to the poor'.

Third, theological education will need to be *multi-mode*, that is, it will need to come out of a cluster of resources where different modes of training from colleges, courses, universities and other agencies are all made available, according to the need of the student. Someone training on a part-time course may need to spend a semester in a college to concentrate his energies on particular topics; someone training in a college may need to spend nine months working in Gateshead using quite different learning methods. Modularisation and credit-transfer will become essential marks of this flexible style of training.

It will also be necessary for theological education to prepare people to be flexible in their approach to ministry, capable of entertaining the possibility of several transmutations in the course of their active service. A lifetime's parochial ministry in single-parish benefices is already a thing of the past. The future may hold a variety of consecutive ministries for a particular priest: first a team vicar working in a church plant; then a sector minister with a team base; then an incumbent with lay ministry teams responsible for each of his local churches; then sharing responsibility for a large city-centre local ecumenical project, and so on. The rapid growth of experiments in ministry, lay and ordained, stipendiary and self-supporting, is an exciting feature of a 'postmodern' Church. But it requires the House of Bishops and the Advisory Board of Ministry to keep a cool head and to intervene with discernment when the Spirit leads the Church to seek order and shape out of the diverse developments. Theological educators will need to be actively preparing students for a ministry of risk and change.

Fourth, training will have to be more *collaborative*. In the first place this applies to methods of teaching and assessment. Is it surprising that so many clergy end up wanting to be 'popes in their own parish', when we teach them to work individualistically, and assess them competitively, with only an occasional foray into the exotic regions of team-teaching and group assessment? Of course, the problem goes far beyond the errors of theological training. The culture of the Church at large is one in which individualism is rewarded and reinforced almost by ecclesial instinct. Considering that the biblical images of the Church are overwhelmingly corporate (the body, the building, the people of God), it is sad that so often clergy are wary of genuine shared ministry, cautious of their neighbours, and reluctant to work together. Congregations often collude with this individualism by rewarding

CORPORATE

personal skill with flattery, and responding enthusiastically to 'strong' leadership or a charismatic personality.

In contrast to this excessive individualism, the Church needs to foster genuine collaboration at all levels. This does not mean that everyone can do everything, that there are no distinctions, unique vocations, particular gifts and ministries. It does mean, on the other hand, that there must be a deeper exploration and understanding of roles in the Church together with a collegial style of work, thought and prayer. Theological training needs to have as a key strategic aim the removal in the Church's future leaders of fear and suspicion of working collaboratively with others. It does not sound much to ask, but it would transform the face of the Church.

Collaborative styles of training are also needed in relation to other agencies of theological education. Our task is but one part of the Christian education of the whole people of God; and I long to see a class in which a part-time Anglican ordinand and a black Methodist lay preacher sit down with a Reader in training and a Roman Catholic priest on sabbatical, to study 1 Corinthians (in Gateshead of course!).

Fifth, our training will have to be *transferable* so that theology doesn't become a hardened deposit of unused material lining the bottom of our mental filing cabinet, but a living resource, used for and with other people in ministry. What people learn they must be able to communicate; and the ways people learn they must be able to use with others. In other words, we must attend to process as well as content. When four young clergy were invited back to their old college to help on a course, they were asked by a wise student what skills they most wish now that they had acquired while at college; and they all answered – skills of adult education. We must have clergy who can communicate; and that includes preaching. Bishop Richard Holloway wrote of preaching recently that much of it 'is a source of enormous pain and boredom to our congregations; and some of it is spiritually damaging to its listeners, because it treats of high and glowing matters, matters of burning importance and absolutely final intent, in a trivial or offhand or inconsequential way'.[1] I recognise it; I've been there; I've listened to myself!

Theological education therefore should be missiological (directed outwards), contextual (relating to specific settings), multi-mode, collaborative, transferable, and doubtless much more besides. We turn now, therefore, to the last and vital question: What then are the possible *scenarios* for theological education in the future, taking account of the problems and applying the principles which have been outlined above?

What are the possible scenarios?

A wise old owl was sitting in the top of a tree when a very worried mouse came scrambling up, with a lion in pursuit on the forest floor. 'What shall I do, owl?' said the mouse frantically. The owl thought for a while. 'You should pluck up your courage, go down, and kill the lion,' pronounced the owl at last. 'You must be joking!' said the mouse. 'Don't blame me,' said the owl, 'I just think out the policy. It's for you to work out the details.'

What detailed scenarios could we consider? The first one would be simple: close the theological colleges. They can't deliver; they can't adapt to a new age; let's cut our losses and invest somewhere else. But to do this would starve ministerial education of the lifeblood of academic theology, which for all its limitations standing alone, must be at the heart of a thinking Church. The colleges are committed to serving the Church with good academic and practical theology; without them the task of sustaining creative theological debate in the Church would be considerably harder. To close the colleges would also mean dismantling theological resources which would be immeasurably more difficult to reconstruct. Moreover, it would speak to the world outside the Church of inexorable decline, giving a further twist to the spiral of despair which some are determined to press upon the Church.

To close the colleges would also frustrate the most academically able of our ordinands who might be left on a parttime course trying to grapple with Moltmann and Pannenberg at the end of an exhausting day's work and doing justice neither to Moltmann nor to themselves. It would also mean losing the value of corporate prayer and life together, the school of theology where ideas are worked out in debate and exchange, in argument and prayer. Close the theological colleges? No – the price is too high.

A second scenario would be for theological education to become parasitic on university departments of theology. Good academic theology could then be supplemented by specific vocational courses and practical placements in vacations, and by short finishing courses where pastoral skills are learned – the continental model. The loss here, however, would be all the gains of the last thirty years which have worked towards the thorough integration of theology and ministry, taking placements with theological seriousness, reflecting on sex and gender as well as systematics, on death and dying as well as Church history. This integration has been hard won; the tide in higher education is with it; we mustn't jettison baby, bathwater and bubble bath all in one go!

The third option is in fact already under way – a regionalised mixed economy with a variety of tracks. There would be a federation or consortium in each region of the country, made up of, for example, a theological college, a course, other denominational agencies, a university faculty of theology, diocesan Boards of Ministry and so on. The federation might then be able to offer four main tracks for ministerial training:

1. A university course, with the federation providing the praxis dimensions through extra modules and supervised placements. Such a course is entirely right for some people; they need to be thoroughly stretched academically, while remaining conscious that the purpose of that theology is ministry. This route should also produce ordinands taking higher degrees who would continue to feed the Church

in theological education, writing and consultancy.

2. The second track would be college-based courses with a 40 per cent praxis component, including a September to Easter placement during one year (three months for a two-year course), and one full day per week in supervised fieldwork. This more regular engagement with the practice of ministry is as essential in ministerial formation as in the formation of nurses or teachers. To tackle the question of suffering in an essay the week after you have sat with a young mother dying of cancer, will produce a much more focused, agonised and valuable response. If more money could be found I would have a three- or four-year course with a whole year in a parish, but I know I cry for the moon! These college-based courses in theology and ministry are nearly in place in many regions; they only need the praxis element upgraded.

3. The third track would be course-based training, using their proven strengths, together with some college modules taught in blocks to focus the input. Courses have demonstrated their ability to take context seriously and to be innovative in teaching and learning methods. The college in the regional federation could add its own expertise with short, intensive modules in particular subject areas. Such modules would be available for all sorts of students, coming to them for a variety of purposes, and thereby enriching the learning community with a variety of backgrounds and needs. When an ordinand sits in a class alongside a priest on sabbatical, not only does he hear different questions from his neighbour, he also finds that he is asking somewhat different questions himself.

4. The fourth track would be the training of local non-stipendiary ministers and local ordained ministers. Such students would use resources from the federation but with a local ministry group to the fore as the main training context. The significant difference here is that the ministry has a local focus and therefore needs to be located within a local group which has responsibility for the mission of the church in its own area. The group would do much of its training together but certain elements and modules would be built in for those

members of groups in whom the Church recognised a call to ordination. The theological argument about local ordained ministry still rages. How can a priest in the Church of God only have a local licence? A priest is a priest is a priest, wherever he or she is! Nevertheless, the Church has always lived with a tension between a universal priesthood and a local expression of that priesthood. It is likely that local ordained ministry or local non-stipendiary ministry will in some form find wide acceptance in the Church of England in the next few years.

The details of all these tracks need not worry us here. Some intelligent mouse would have to do a lot of work! The point now is to recognise the potential of a mixed economy where a single vision for theological education is expressed in a variety of interdependent tracks.

Theological colleges will have to change or go to the wall. They will have to be flexible, open systems, offering educational modules of high quality and clear focus, but all within an ongoing life of worship and resurrection-faith. A college is not a supermarket; many good things are packed on its shelves, but it stays open long after the trolleys have been locked away. Its heart is in bearing witness to a way of being together in Christ, in order to form men and women who are spiritually alive, theologically thoughtful and pastorally wise. Ministry involves more than being a spiritual technician; it's about being a Christlike person, and ordained ministry is about being a Christlike person with a special representative focus. The task of a theological college is to produce this kind of person; they aren't found on shelves: they grow.

What is more, these clergy are an essential resource for the Church and need to be valued as such, cherished rather than squandered. This is not to make a higher claim for ordained ministry than for lay; it is simply to recognise difference, and the particular contribution of a skilled, self-aware and prayerful presbyterate in the life of the Church at this very crucial time. The marginalisation of the Church in contemporary society can leave clergy feeling particularly exposed, and the answer lies in going deeper into the nature of God and of priesthood, rather than in retreating into a more secular model of managerial priests.

I was returning home by train from a meeting of bishops and others involved in theological education at which fine and important strategies had been discussed in an articulate and nuanced way. Next to me on the train was a woman with a lively eight year old. Favouring anonymity and fearing discovery I kept my nose in my book, but unfortunately it was theological, and the woman noticed and was clearly curious. At last I was flushed out and a conversation started up. She was a single mother returning from a visit to the nun who had particularly influenced her when she was brought up in a children's home years before. A chord of need had been struck, a deep resonance sounded. Should she go to church, she wondered, and if so, which one? Perhaps it would be better to try the Church of England because – she asked this rather non-plussed Anglican clergyman – 'you don't have to go to church every week there, do you?' Her daughter proudly produced a little book of prayers the nun had just given her. It contained the rosary and 'the nice little prayer' (the Lord's Prayer). 'What do you think I should do?' asked the woman.

What the woman did not need was my strategic thinking on theological education in the Church of England. She did not need this church bureaucrat trying to avoid being noticed, a manager of ecclesiastical resources happy in his own world. She needed directing to a down-to-earth God. She needed a visible sign of God's commitment to her, such as she had recognised in a nun who years before had made God real to her in practical deeds of love and care. She needed someone who represented and embodied a life of sacrificial action rooted in the sacrificial life of Jesus Christ. The shape of Christian priesthood, lay and ordained, will have to be distinctively formed by the radical life and sacrifice of Christ. It will be the quality of that living, undergirded by the reality of prayer and rooted in the mystery of an absurdly generous God, that will reveal the integrity of a person's ministry. A priest who is part therapist and part manager will simply not do.

At its best a theological college is a powerhouse of intellectual and spiritual energy for the whole Church. To close down such a power source would be to condemn the Church to a still more desperate struggle against the darkness. To use a college well is to generate light to fill the lives of thousands of 'women-on-the-train' with the empowering, liberating love of God.

6

The ministry of laity

David Day

David Day is Principal of St John's College, Durham

I suppose we should know better but it still sounds odd to speak of being called to be a layperson. Those who bewail 'falling numbers of vocations' are nearly always referring to the supply of ordinands. The laity is that body of people out of which you are called. They may also be defined as the 'not-clergy'. Half-mended nets, tent-making and the receipt of custom are the things you leave behind when you hear the call and (in an extraordinary phrase) 'go into the church'. Does it make sense to speak of a vocation to be a layperson?

And yet . . . fourteen years ago the Council of St John's, Durham, made history by appointing the first female layperson to be head of an Anglican theological college. To this day Ruth Etchells still describes herself as 'unrepentantly a member of the laity'. To whatever ministry she was called it was not that of the ordained, nor is it so even now when such a translation has become possible. To speak personally for a moment, one of my most treasured possessions is a volume of Kierkegaard given to me by a friend after I had decided not to seek ordination. It bears the inscription: 'To David, as a sort of non-ordination present, celebrating your decision not to be different but to be a Christian in the middle of things'. For my friend and for Dr Etchells it seems as though it is possible to conceive of the laity, no less than the clergy, as being summoned to an important and valuable ministry.

In fact, on reflection, we do not have much of a problem here. It is clear that the laity are called, by virtue of being Christ's disciples, to be the people of God. They are to be the body of Christ in any given place. There they are to exercise a royal priesthood. This is their vocation since it is the common vocation of all who are baptised. Their Christian discipleship, as always, will be primarily worked out in the world. In practice this is precisely what happens. The laity bring the world with its concerns, its pressures, its incoherences, its ambiguities and its pain into the worship and prayer of the Church – and, if all goes as it should, they then go back into that world to follow Christ 'in the middle of things'. The point is well made in some words of Archbishop Carey:

> The centre of God's mission . . . (is) not the splendid work of Church life but the equally splendid wilderness of the world . . . where there are few places for Christians to hide, where moral and ethical signposts are blurred or non-existent and where we are outnumbered by the indifferent, the unholy and the cultured despisers of our day.[1]

The primary vocation is to follow Christ; the world is the primary locus of God's mission.

It looks as if the problem with which I started has turned upside down. If the fundamental truth about vocation and ministry is as I have stated it above, then anything which blurs that truth ought to be strenuously resisted. There is one calling from Christ, obeyed and expressed in a variety of ways and within a variety of situations but essentially the same – 'Follow me'. Any sharp distinction between clergy and laity is likely to obscure the central point. Clergy, not less than laity, are called to be members of the people of God and the body of Christ. The idea of a 'second call' is part of a long and honourable tradition but it is not linked with a 'higher call' to a superior way of life or ministry. Such a connection is in effect potentially very damaging.

Unfortunately, within the Church of England as we know it and despite frequent calls to 'liberate the laity', the distinction between ordained and lay has tended to be over-emphasised and has been less than beneficial in its result. Over the years it has helped to produce a clericalisation of the Church. It has encouraged the idea that the laity are in some sense second class. Against the biblical notion that the priest is there to help the laity do their job, it has persuaded the laity that their role is to help the priest do his job. George Carey comments again:

> Ministry is dislocated by the creation of a professional caste who are different from lay Christians because they know 'how to do' things. Without any question a form of mystique has formed around the ordained minister, leaving an unfortunate legacy in ill-equipped lay Christians unused to using their gifts in Christian service. It is not too sweeping to say that the majority of priests and ministers today . . . do not know how to give ministry back to the congregation.[2]

These two features of contemporary Anglican life, the reaffirmation of the ministry of the laity and the deleterious effects of clericalisation, have become significant elements in a number of recent debates, not least those to do with the nature of mission and the future of the parish system. In the summer of 1994 they surfaced in a General Synod debate on eucharistic presidency. The possibility of lay people presiding at Holy Communion raised the issue of the respective roles of lay and ordained in a peculiarly sharp manner. Could the Church of England agree on a theology of ministry? And ought a church which claimed to take lay ministry seriously permit this new development, even though recognising that it would mark a break with tradition?

Of course, the discussion calls for some kind of definition of what might count as 'lay presidency'. It is a slippery term which can cover a range of situations. At one end of the continuum it might allow any layperson to preside with (or worse still, without) the invitation of the incumbent. This was the 'free-for-all' feared by many and seen as a recipe for anarchy. In fact, a good deal of heat was generated by the suggestion that 'every Tom, Dick and Harry, Karen, Mary and Anne can go forward and administer the sacraments'. At the other end it might describe some kind of formal authorisation by the bishop along the lines of the licensing of Readers. Lay presidents would then be episcopally authorised, likely to hold some kind of leadership position within a congregation, exercising their presidency only within that congregation and doing so only occasionally. Between the free-for-all and this much more restricted understanding there lie numerous permutations and possibilities which are yet further complicated by the question of whether the presidency might be exercised in the absence or only in the presence of the incumbent.

However, even the cautious version of what is entailed is enough to constitute a threat for many people. They hold that the real objection to lay presidency is that it undermines precious truths to do with priesthood and Eucharist. Chris McGillion writing in *The Tablet* complained, 'if lay presidency is introduced, the role, meaning and definition of priesthood becomes confused'.[3] Certainly, Synod was left in no doubt that lay presidency was a threat to Anglican order. Ecclesiastical and theological heavyweights queued up to express their disagreement. The Archbishop of Canterbury described the proposal as 'unnecessary, unwelcome, untimely and unAnglican'; the Archbishop of York thought the proposer 'on a hiding to nothing' and the Bishop of Ely considered lay presidency 'incompatible with Anglican tradition'.

In the face of such comments I am clearly in the wrong company and it may be sensible to give up before beginning. However, episcopal and archiepiscopal opposition notwithstanding, it is still worth trying to show that there are good grounds for allowing lay presidency in certain carefully prescribed situations. I am aware that there is profound disagreement between those on either side of the issue. Different theologies, different presuppositions, different authorities . . . when the elephant meets the whale common ground is hard to come by. Where there is no meeting of minds on the ground of basic principles one is sometimes reduced to making affirmation do the job of argument. Nevertheless, I still wish to set out, in as non-confrontational a way as possible, some of the reasons which lead me to favour lay presidency.

The silence of Scripture

It is not possible to find in the New Testament any indication of who presided at the common meal. Attempts have been made to draw analogies with presidency at different types of Jewish meals but the argument is at best highly speculative. In fact, if the model of eucharistic presidency was drawn from Jewish grace at meals then, according to Schillebeeckx, anyone could preside. The plain fact is that Scripture says nothing definite on the subject. It is, therefore, at least possible to argue that it is silent because the question of who presided was not an issue and was not particularly important. Common sense would lead us to suppose that an elder would preside but if we throw in the fact that eldership within a local congregation appears always to have been plural then it is very difficult by that route to get to the characteristic Anglican practice of one priest always presiding.

The tradition of the Church

The rule that only bishops and presbyters may preside is extremely ancient. We shall not get much support from tradition. Nevertheless there are examples in the *Didache* where prophets are allowed to celebrate; they preside at the Eucharist and may formulate the eucharistic prayer in a free way but 'in the Spirit' (Did 10.7,15). Schillebeeckx makes the interesting point that 'in the earliest stratum of the *Didache* the prophets and teachers preside at the eucharist'. It is only 'in a later stratum they are joined by presbyters and deacons who do so by virtue of their office'.[4] It seems as if exercising a teaching ministry was seen as a mark of leadership and therefore a qualification for presidency. In a contemporary context this practice would certainly justify extending presidency to a wider circle than that of the ordained priesthood.

In another suggestive passage, Hippolytus seems to imply that confessors who have suffered for the faith without actually dying, may be declared to be presbyters without laying-on of hands. Tertullian maintains that in the absence of clergy, laypersons are allowed to celebrate. The effect of passages like these is at least to raise questions about rigid rules of ordination and eucharistic monopoly. Do they leave the door open just half an inch?

In any case, tradition remains tradition. Church history is full of examples of development where the Church has modified tradition while remaining faithful to the original gospel insights. To insist on tradition for tradition's sake is understandable but ultimately indefensible. It amounts to saying, 'Because that's the way we do it in Anglicanism. So there!' In the debate on lay presidency in the Sydney Diocese one speaker came very close to this. The Dean of St Andrew's Cathedral argued: 'My objection is principally one of order, of how we do things, of how we have agreed to set things up, of our understanding of ordination. The Church of England has decided that priests should celebrate Holy Communion. It could have chosen otherwise, but it did not.' But a Church which has seen the admission of women to the ordained priesthood can hardly treat tradition as unchangeable. Tradition promises continuity with the past but not in a literalistic or mechanical way. In itself tradition is a neutral term. We have to ask whether the tradition serves the gospel or not.

The gospel community

I have already argued that it is the nature of the gospel community, insofar as it is predominantly a lay community, to work out its vocation in 'the wilderness of the world'. Roger Tiller and Mark Birchall underline this fact: 'Christians at first made no distinction between service of God in the world and worship of God in a building. In fact service and worship are the same idea: it was in their daily work and witness that they offered their sacrifices.'[5] I do not wish to imply by this quotation that daily work can supplant what the New Testament means by assembling together. Nevertheless, in the Synod debate much was made of what the Eucharist symbolised and in what sense the president acted in a representative capacity. Occasional lay presidency would bring a new dimension to the worship of the Church; it would bring the context of Christ's work into sharp focus. For it would ensure that the congregation, for that occasion, was led in its worship by one who was daily and routinely having to draw upon the riches of Christ in order 'to live and work to his praise and glory' *in the world*. The president for this occasion would preserve this insight precisely by being a layperson.

The role of the priest

From the perspective of role definition it is easy to argue that the rediscovery of the ministry of the laity has left the priest with nothing to do except absolve, bless and consecrate at communion. Psychologically one can understand the loss of identity which many priests feel. As the laity take over more and more of the priest's role so it becomes yet more important to make a last-ditch stand. 'You can have everything else but this one right you will not have. This is the essence of being a priest.' Hence there is a tendency to define the role of the priest almost exclusively in terms of a eucharistic ministry; but this is an unnecessary and undesirable outcome. Why should a sacramental ministry be seen as the essence of being a priest and not, say, the preaching ministry or the pastoral ministry? The command to 'Feed my sheep' need not, and ought not, to be taken to refer exclusively or even primarily to the Eucharist. There are aspects of the priestly ministry which are devalued by an excessive concentration on eucharistic presidency as its raison d'etre. Extending the presidency of the Eucharist to lay people under certain carefully defined conditions would not take this privilege away from the priesthood. It might help the Church to see more clearly the multidimensional ministry of the priest.

The symbolism of the Eucharist

Clericalisation of the Church has distorted the way the Eucharist is understood. It is perilously easy to see the service as something which the president does. This has two effects. First, the truth that this liturgy is the offering of the whole people of God is obscured. 'Celebrant' is not a helpful word. The priest does not celebrate. The whole people of God celebrate. It is 'the bread which *we* break . . .' There are many ways of representing Christ at the Eucharist. Against the concept of the priest as the icon, image or representative of Christ, we might set the view that the president is the representative of the congregation. And then it is the congregation which is the body or icon of Christ.

Second, the heart of the Eucharist tends to be located primarily in the prayer of consecration and what happens to the bread and the wine and not in the liturgy taken as a whole. Benedict Green, though not sharing my view of lay presidency, yet has this helpful observation to make.

> The eucharist is an action – more strictly a sequence of actions of which communion is the climax. To divorce it from what has led up to it is to risk obscuring that it is about the death and resurrection of Christ and that our communion with him (and in him, with one another) rests on our reconciliation to God through him.[6]

The Eucharist is a sequence of actions and it is in the service taken as a whole, in ministry of the Word, prayers, the peace, the thanksgiving, the communion and so on, in the great story and rhythm of the liturgy that its significance rests. Focus on what are sometimes irreverently called 'the magic words' and you lose that truth. But, as things stand at present, the necessary presence of a priest 'to say the magic words', virtually the only part which may not be taken by a layperson, gives disproportionate weight to one movement within the total action.

The oversight of the congregation

It has been fairly conclusively established that eldership or oversight in the New Testament was plural and corporate. This was certainly the case in the charismatic communities of Paul. They lived by the conviction that Christ had given gifts to the Church, which included gifts of leadership, and that those gifts had been recognised by the community under the illumination of the Spirit. There was, however, no sense that any one person had a monopoly of all the gifts. There is no place in the New Testament for the omnicompetent vicar (still less for the omni-incompetent vicar). Leadership in the local church is to be corporate and plural. Unhappily, this insight has been largely lost, and attempts to argue that it is preserved in combinations like vicar and curate or bishop and diocesan clergy are a fudge. The World Council of Churches in a statement on 'Baptism, Eucharist and Ministry' put the position with masterly understatement: '. . . in some churches the collegial dimension of leadership . . . has suffered diminution.'[7] You might indeed say so! If leadership is supposed to be collegial, lay presidency will do something to restore that truth by embodying it in the Eucharist.

The analogy with preaching the Word

I suggested above that the clericalisation of the Church has led inevitably to an extreme emphasis on the sacramental. This is seen par excellence as the place where God encounters the congregation. So Holy Communion gets elevated as a kind of super-sacrament. Sometime this has been accompanied by a reduction in the importance of the sermon; a five-minute homily will do in order to get on quickly to the really important part. I do not wish to argue for very long sermons simply to make a point, but preaching is not a second best. The Bishop of Edinburgh has argued that Word and sacrament are both places where Christ is present, where he speaks and encounters us:

> I'm fond of Bernard Manning's definition of preaching as
> 'the manifestation of the incarnate word from the written
> word through the spoken word'. Incidentally this may
> be one reason why traditions that have a high view of
> preaching frequently have a lower view of the Eucharist,
> because they experience the real presence of Christ in the
> sermon and encounter him there. It may also be why
> traditions that have a high doctrine of the real presence
> in the Eucharist often have a low appreciation of his real
> presence in preaching. It seems to me, however, that to
> be truly catholic and evangelical we must cleave to the
> doctrine that Christ is manifested in word and sacrament,
> and probably only fully when they are married together.[8]

When a preacher has heard a word within God's silence and speaks it into the life of the congregation then things happen, people are stopped in their tracks, the fire falls, lives are changed, 'the Spirit breathes upon the word and brings the truth to life'. This is a high view of preaching. It is one shared by the Archbishop of York when he described preaching as 'a vitally important and terrifying thing to do'. But if this is so, on what grounds can we permit lay people to speak the Word and forbid them to administer the sacrament?

I am told that the analogy will not hold. I am stubborn enough to say that I cannot see why not. Both Word and sacrament are places where God encounters us. We allow lay people, properly authorised and trained, to preach the Word. Why can they not preside at the common meal? In the Synod debate Dr Habgood suggested that it was because preaching was largely functional, 'although it has some representational aspects'. Celebrating the Eucharist, on the other hand, 'is not just a function, it is basically about representing the whole church'. I am not sure that I am convinced by this. If the priest in presiding at this local celebration is in some sense representing not just the congregation but also the whole church then no less is the preacher who dares to speak in the name of God and out of the 'faith once delivered to the saints'. A preacher dare not just represent himself or herself. He or she does not speak for this tiny bit of the Church – 'what I, or I and my friends, believe'. If it is really a ministry of the Word, then preaching is as representative an activity as presiding at the Eucharist.

The inadequacy of alternatives

I end where others begin, with the practical problems posed by our present situation. Unwillingness to allow lay presidency has resulted in makeshift solutions which solve nothing and are in some cases dishonouring to the gospel. What is so glorious about the harassed incumbent who is compelled to drive furiously around the district in order to get communion to eight different churches and confesses himself 'massed out' at the end of the day? What system of pastoral care denies a rural congregation their weekly communion because there is no priest to deliver it? Worse still, what theory of nurture and follow-up insists that congregations of new Christians in South America and Africa have to make do with communion once a year for want of a priest? Would the communities of the early Church have produced such a system? Why must communion cease when the priest falls ill or goes on holiday? How can 'the care of souls' demand that a priest be imported who has absolutely no pastoral relationship at all with the congregation? In all our talk of representation, exactly what is being represented here? When will congregations query the adequacy of reserved sacrament or extended communion which focus Christ in the elements and not in the whole meal? All these are desperate expedients, which give out harmful signals and obscure significant aspects of the gospel.

These are some of the reasons which lead me to support lay presidency. It should be clear that they are not primarily to do with practicalities. Nor are they motivated by a desire to provoke Anglo-Catholics or rock the ecclesiastical ark. They have their basis in theology, spirituality and ecclesiology.

Nor do I believe that lay presidency irreparably damages or confuses the concept of the ordained ministry. The discovery that leadership in the Church means shared leadership, in shared ministry of the Word and in shared ministry of the sacraments does not mean that the presbyterial office has been evacuated of all content. When Jesus shared his ministry with the twelve and with the seventy his authority was not diminished in any way.

In fact, the role of the priest is as demanding and vital as it always has been. He or she is an elder, called to be the leader of the mission of the people of God. Schillebeeckx comments, 'no matter what form it takes ministry is concerned with the leadership of the community: ministers are pioneers, those who inspire the community and serve as models by which the whole community can identify the gospel'.[9] As pioneers and models priests will continue to have a representative function. They will represent the congregation to the wider Church and represent the wider Church within the congregation. There should be no loss of identity or role here.

It should be obvious by now that I do not support lay presidency in order to disparage or downgrade the role of the priest. Nor, I hope, am I exhibiting the characteristic evangelical delight in debunking inherited practices. My motives are rather

more constructive. I want the life which the Church lives in the
world to be brought into the heart of the Church's worship;
I want the clericalisation of the Church to be supplanted
by the multicoloured grace of God; I want the preached
Word once again to stand alongside the enacted Word. Occasional, properly authorised lay presidency will embody and
express all these great truths.

When Dr John Woodhouse introduced the motion on Lay
Presidency at the Sydney Diocesan Synod, he called it 'a
responsible, cautious, conservative, non-confrontational and
thoroughly orderly step forward'. One might suppose that the
next move should be to prosecute the case with vigour and
launch the campaign without delay. In fact I think such a
course of action at this time would have disastrous consequences for the Church. It would cause untold pain and
distress. Frankly, the price is too high. But the arguments
should be allowed to run freely and the issue given its proper
place in debate and report. It is my hope that in due time the
Church will accept lay presidency. Meanwhile, let us pursue
all that makes for peace and builds up the common life.

7

The ministry of women

Margaret Masson

Margaret Masson lectures in English Literature, is a writer, and
is Senior Tutor at St John's College, Durham

In my recent reading and thinking, I have been forced to
confront the possibility more seriously than I ever have before
that maybe the Church is, after all, irretrievably patriarchal.
Perhaps women should not be fighting to join the higher
echelons of its power. Do we really want to identify ourselves so centrally with an institution in which women have
been demeaned for centuries? With an institution which still,
despite some token gestures here and there, seems so very
reluctant, so terribly fearful of bringing us into the heart of
its life? Should women continue to bolster such a system? To
legitimate, by agreeing to be priests or bishops, what might
be a fundamentally dysfunctional order? This is a perspective
that many women who are members of the Anglican Church
in England must face from their feminist friends and indeed
from their own sense of exclusion within the liturgies and
sensibilities and hierarchies of the established Church.

What if these voices are right? What if the idea of women
bishops is indeed unthinkable? As contrary voices pull us
hither and thither, how do we begin to find a way through
the web of controversial issues? There are three aspects of
the Christian tradition that might help us to untangle some
of what is at stake here: the Bible; the language, imagery and
symbolism of the Christian tradition; and the structures and
shape of the institutional Church itself.

The Bible

To be a Christian, one must surely have some belief in the authority of Christianity's Holy Scripture: it is the foundational Christian text. And many of those who would object to women being ordained priests and bishops, base their views on undeniably biblical notions of male headships, authority and oversight. Indeed, it is very hard to argue that the Bible does not support a basically patriarchal view of authority and leadership. One could produce endless stories and proof-texts – from Adam and Eve to the Apostle Paul – where men's leadership and authority over women is either implicitly accepted or clearly argued.

Feminist biblical critics such as Phyllis Trible[1] have done impressive and valuable work in deconstructing some of this patriarchal idealogy which seems indelibly inscribed into so many biblical texts. Trible and others have suggested that there is often a subversive subtext in Bible narratives that implodes into an interpretation that reads utterly against the grain of the traditional assumptions of a male-centred perspective. The very way in which the Bible has traditionally been read means that its readers fail to grasp the critique it carries within it, a critique of abusive male power exposed and condemned. When read with Trible's careful sensitivity to the woman's perspective, the Bible is indeed far kinder to women than we have been taught to believe.

This is certainly a valuable approach. It is important to draw attention to the forgotten women of the Bible and to look more closely at the plight of the injured ones. But can this line of argument really rescue the Bible from the charge that it inspires a religion of and for men? For every text, every story, every woman thus rescued, there must be a dozen others whose treatment it is very hard to reinterpret so generously. Is it not ultimately futile, even quixotic, to try and retrieve the Bible from the charge of patriarchalism? On the question of the authority of the Holy Scripture, must we not agree that the idea of women bishops is unthinkable?

Language, imagery and symbolism

In these more aesthetic realms of nuance and subtle possibility, can Christian women find more joy? Unfortunately, one only has to spend five minutes in the average service of Christian worship to have to concede the fact that the language of the Church is far from inclusive of women. There is, in general, scant attempt to resist sexist language. In hymns, in psalms, in prayers, in translations of the Bible and even in sermons, we find ourselves absorbing the imagery of battles and kings, of fathers and brothers and sons, of men and lords, slaves and masters, of ordering and subduing and conquering . . . it is not that these are not sometimes appropriate images, or even imaginatively instructive. It is the fact that in overwhelming numbers they seem to have a very masculine universe in mind, that they consistently refer to men and not women, to 'his' and 'him', to good Christian men and 'mankind' and brethren, and so create little space for women near the centre of any service.

So, as they try to worship, too many women are left angry, frustrated and distracted. Attempting to redeem the offending text or image in mid-flow, it is hard not to be inwardly resentful of the complacency of the men around them who sing and recite blithely on, oblivious to the discomfort of their seeing sisters. The language of the Church is certainly not, in the context of the late twentieth-century Western world, welcoming to women. The sensibility which is forged, encouraged and reinforced by such language works powerfully against any attempt to lay a foundation for women having a place at the centre of the Church's official life along with men.

But there is a more fundamental objection to any attempt to legitimate the notion of women being near the centre of the Church's images of authority, its symbols of salvation. Crucial to Christian symbolism and meaning is a male Christ. Once again, the traditionalists and the post-Christian feminists find themselves in unlikely alliance. Christ is the exact representation of God, the image of God's very self. It is surely no accident, so both camps would argue, that God became incarnate as a male. Indeed, one of the most important image clusters in the Christian faith depends on the masculinity of Christ: he is the heavenly bridegroom and the Church is his bride. In the rich imagery of Christian eschatology, heaven is described in terms of the marriage feast of the Lamb. Wouldn't this imagery – absolutely central to the celebration of the Eucharist – collapse if Christ's representative were female? Here again, we must surely concede that the notion of women bishops representing this male Christ is unthinkable.

Church structures and institution

The structures of the institution of the Church itself are surely more susceptible to adaptation and change than either the Bible or the Church's symbols might be. Is it possible that in the Church institutional, the idea of women's headship need not be unthinkable? After all, institutions are largely the work of human agency: it is in their nature to change. Yet why is it that so often, religious institutions seem far more resistant to change, far more conservative, than secular ones? There seems to be something in the religious sensibility that is drawn towards security, order, establishment, continuity. This is not, of course, necessarily a bad thing; after all, we ritualise and reify that which we most care about as well as that which we most fear. But it is not particularly good news for women who long for a more positive role in the Church.

Throughout the ages, women have not had a good press within the Christian tradition. As Christianity became infected with gnostic notions of dualism – so at odds with the remarkably earthy, materialistic faith of the Jews and the incarnated Jesus – women suffered in the resulting distortions. Often identified with the body, with sexuality, with nature, they came to represent those aspects of being that men found it so very hard to keep in order. Some of this obsessive fear of losing control has been ritualised and structured into the very fabric of the Church. And the deep-seated wariness of women, for various reasons, remains. Is there much, then, to give us grounds to argue for women bishops from the tradition?

Might it be that these objections of Bible, symbolism, institutionalism really are insurmountable? If so, the post-Christian feminists may be right: not only is there no room for women bishops in the Church. Perhaps there is no room for women.

And yet, and yet . . . at the very core of the Christian faith is the doctrine of grace, the bedrock belief that God will not be limited by our feeble human strictures and constraints whether of interpretation or imagination or institutions. We cannot, we dare not, take things at face value. Faith teaches us that things are not always as they seem.

So, back to the Bible. The defenders of slavery once called upon the Bible to support their case. The verses and examples are still there. Polygamy – still defensible in some cultures, but not to most of us – has a respectable pedigree in the Bible. Levitical food laws that most of us would not dream of trying to keep, acts of vindictiveness and revenge that many a twentieth-century sensibility finds appalling . . . it's all there in the Bible. The Church now condemns many of the customs and assumptions that the great patriarchs took for granted. We are constantly revising what discipleship to God means in this time and culture, continually reconsidering what in this day and age constitutes sin. The revelation we receive is never wholly separable from human culture, from human interpretation.

This is not to water down the demands of the faith or even, by the grace of God, to pick and choose whatever suits us. It is to grasp the reality that ours is not a static faith which consists of abiding by time-bound rules, but a prophetic faith that depends constantly on the indwelling Spirit of God to keep us in love and obedience with God's very Self.

The Bible is God's Word as Jesus is God's Word. In both revelations, God took the supreme risk of incarnation, and one of the glorious truths of the Christian gospel is that God's Word risks human particularity. In both revelations to humanity, the Word became flesh. Flesh is organic, not mechanical; its shape and meaning is not static, fixed like a beautiful but lifeless marble statue for all time, but, more like a Shakespearean play, fluid and densely textured with a depth and range of meaning that it is the task and delight of generation after generation to discover and discern and act out afresh.

The fact that many texts or passages in the Bible seem to discourage women's leadership, then, is not argument enough for today's Church. The very spirit of the gospel which brings us salvation by faith and through a living relationship rather than through rules laid down and blueprints to be followed, demands otherwise. As Christians, we have no option but to interpret our faith in the light of the culture in which we live. And if the ethical imperative of our time can no longer justify the exclusion of marginal groups from particular offices or responsibilities, we cannot ignore it.

Is this just pandering to the transient dictates of an ephemeral cultural trend? Yet not to pay attention equally risks the idolatry of ossifying, even deifying, one particular hermeneutical principle, one way of understanding what constitutes legitimate Christian leadership. It is to risk a cipher view of revelation that leads quickly to bibliolatry and the temptation to live by the dead letter and not the living spirit.

But, returning to our second contentious area, what of the problem of the sexist language that still riddles the Church's official texts and liturgies? Is such language inevitable, irresistible, inescapable? Are feminist women in the Church doomed to generations of liturgy that fails to take seriously their discomfort at being linguistically excluded? Yet, some would argue, the debate about inclusive language is far from over and it is therefore unfair to freeze and judge it at a particular moment in time. Much of the language now heard as excluding women was not intended to do so. It is only comparatively

recently that the use of 'man' as generic has been questioned and challenged. The English language is indeed in
a state of confusion and transition over the issue of sexist
language. It may indeed, then, be premature to castigate the
Church for simply reflecting the language that is still the
common parlance of most people.

So, if the case is made for inclusive language – and many
thoughtful people have their doubts about whether it is desirable or important – perhaps it is unfair to expect the Church to
be ahead of its culture in this area. This leads us into the kind
of debate about language, and about the role of the Church
as representative or prophetic within its culture, to which we
have no time to do justice here. Suffice it to state here my
own belief: that our cultural linguistic sensibility has changed
and is changing. What used to be construed as generic, and
was not intended to be gender clusive, now feels different.
It has a new set of associations and an altered significance
which does give offence to an increasing number of women.
The Church cannot ignore this or hope that the fad will
soon pass. Its tardiness will be excused only for so long.

This said, I am happy to concede that there is some very
encouraging work being done writing liturgies, hymns and
translating the Bible in ways which are sensitive to women's
needs and perspectives and which make an effort to appropriate the feminine imagery that already exists within the
tradition.[2] In time, then, it is possible that the official texts of
the Church will be rendered more inclusive. And, given the
way in which language determines the way in which we
understand ourselves and perceive the way things are, the
Church may indeed gradually develop a sensibility that is
more likely to be able to imagine women as bishops.

The problem of the particular symbolism of a male Christ is
harder to overcome. After all, that Jesus was male is nowhere,
as far as I know, disputed. What about the image of Christ
as heavenly bridegroom? Isn't his masculinity here vitally significant? In response, I would first ask: who decides and how
do they decide which aspects of Christ's human particularity

are significant and which are not? Jesus was not only male, he was also a Jew from Palestine and the son of a carpenter. Why, in determining who may and may not represent him, is the factor of his sex all-important?

But conceding for a moment that it might be: is the leap of imagination needed to cope with a female representing the bridegroom so very much greater than the leap of each male member of the Church in identifying as the Bride? Is it any more confusing to imagine, as the tradition in various places suggests, Christ's bride-mother born from his own wounded side, or the Son's role in the Trinity being described in terms of self-giving surrender, the one who allows himself to be led and fertilised by the Father throughout his earthly ministry?[3] Far from rigid gender roles, there is much in the tradition of Christian symbolism that would suggest a remarkable degree of gender fluidity. Jesus is no merely male blueprint, and human inclusive salvation demands that he should not be, if women too are deemed to be represented by his humanity.

This whole area of gender identity is, of course, fiercely contested ground in the late twentieth-century West. Is our gender identity – our masculinity, our femininity – a 'given', fixed once and for all in the creation ordinance? Or is it something which is more a matter of human culture playing out variations on God's themes? Our argument about the significance of gender here might be similar to those about how we read Scripture: is it – Scripture, gender – a blueprint for living or improvisation around key themes? If the latter is the case, perhaps Jesus' maleness is not, after all, a stumbling block to the notion of women bishops.

So, revisiting our third category, the institution of the Church. Is it possible within the tradition of hostility towards women in Christian history that here too there might be room for hope? I remember a few years ago sitting in an auditorium in the college where I taught in the States, listening to a white British orator hauntingly lamenting the fragmentation of Western culture, the lost cohesion of our Christian heritage. I happened to look across to a black colleague, sitting with his head in his hands. What was he making of all this? Was this Christian past so glorious in his eyes? What did he have to be so nostalgic about? His great-grandfathers subjected to the humiliations of the slave auctions, prodded and poked by prospective buyers? His great-grandmothers raped at whim by their white masters? We need to be careful when arguing the claims of the past. Whose past? Whose tradition? Whose glory?

Tradition can be bad as much as it can be good. This is our responsibility, and we are capable of carrying forward what is oppressive and stultifying every bit as much as what is life-giving and salvific. Jesus' gospel of the coming of the kingdom of God often challenges us precisely on the axis of tradition/transformation. It is our longing for security, for knowing exactly where we are in the scheme of things that can so easily lead to the shaping of a fixed religion which spares us the effort of having to be continually re-sponsive to the dynamic spirit of the living God. And in such stasis lie the roots of idolatry, of the comfortable but ultimately deathly temptation of giving our all to something less than God, and thereby stifling our humanity. Arguing from tradition, then, we dare not simply conclude that the idea of women bishops is taboo.

So, can a case now be made? On the basis of our look at these three main areas of Christian identity: the Bible, Christian symbolism and the institution of the Church, are we ready for the triumphant peroration? Unfortunately, not quite! It is far from certain that even if women were to become bishops, it would make any real difference to the Church. Some committed Christian feminists argue against the move of women's ordination for just this reason. They fear that, far from helping to transform the Church, women will just be co-opted into existing structures and practices, that they will be 'clericalised' and simply reinforce patterns so rooted in hierarchical authoritarianism and a sensibility of exclusion that nothing will change. Or, worse, that complacency and injustice will just flourish in less overt, more insidious ways.

There are important debates about the whole system of priesthood and bishophood. Does it, as one Roman Catholic writer suggests, simply pander to our paganism?[4] Or, as one black woman priest in the States asks, does it just satisfy our craving for 'little gods',[5] thereby relieving most of us of the responsibility for our own relationship with God, our own contribution to Christ's Church here on earth, our own 'traditioning'? But these are arguments for another time. I raise them here merely as a caution against too easy an advocacy for women bishops. The dangers are very real.

Yet once again, I am forced to acknowledge that in a world view in which the grace of God is fundamental, cynicism is not a final option. I do believe that if women move into high office in the Church, transformation may gradually result. The very fact that women have been marginalised in the Church over centuries has presumably bred into many of us an ambivalence about power and authority. At the very least, this may inspire us to question patterns of power within the Church, possibly even help to reconceive it.

The Amish, that family of Christians we often find quaint in their refusal to move with the times and dress like we do and use machines like we do, have some wise thoughts on power. The reason they do not permit tractors in their fields is not just because they are stubbornly stuck in a time warp. If you use a hand plough, you are close enough to what you are doing to see the soil as it is churned up and broken apart. You are not cut off, protected from the effect of your action as you would be in a tractor. This intimacy breeds gentleness. Our own violence is overlooked when the reverberations of our actions are remote from us. Women have generally been far from the centres of power in the Church, they are more likely to have been at the receiving end of the effects of remotely executed power than to have been its perpetrators. With this visceral experience of their own marginality, they just might be more likely to bring (for just as long as they remember their experience on the edge of things) a certain gentleness and inclusiveness into the practice of power, authority, and leadership in the Church. Equally, they will have to learn the endurance necessary to exercise publicly accountable responsibility.

And there is the further possibility that if women become bishops, the nature of the role itself will have to change. Women tend to be much less willing than men to let their identities, their lives, revolve exclusively around their work. And if they are mothers, or responsible – as so many women are – for the care of the fragile and vulnerable, the kind of workaholism that too often characterises those in high office would simply not be practical: it certainly is not desirable. In a world where some people are absurdly busy and disproportionately important whilst others are made to feel insignificant and can find no way to contribute to the common good, might women in church leadership show us the way towards sharing the load and the sense of mattering in the scheme of things?

If women's leadership really is taken seriously, there would have to be a greater number of bishops to help carry out the work, and perhaps the true pastoral nature of the bishop's office would come once again to be felt to be as important as its power. Could women bishops also help to challenge our capitalist notion of vocation, in which persons are understood as economic units, and help to restore the notion of human beings as 'called ones'?

These, of course, are not just women's issues. Women's ministry, women's leadership, women's authority, is also about so much more. These questions raise other, deeper questions about why certain categories of people are excluded from or disapproved of in the ordained Anglican ministry – not only on the basis of gender, but also of class, education, colour or sexuality. Why should this be? All the arguments about women bishops might well apply to other categories of people. Might they also suggest, for example, why the Church is so nervous about admitting homosexual people to the centre of its life in late twentieth-century Britain?

Is this phenomenon of exclusion simply a part of our human need to set up systems within which we feel comfortable and which we can control? Perhaps such systems demand that there are 'others', those outside our group, beyond the pale, against whom we can define ourselves as righteous, normal, God's true representatives. And so we feel powerful, in control. But the setting up of such watertight systems of exclusion, of resisting what is culturally or religiously taboo, while it may indeed be faithfulness to God, may equally be a form of idolatry. It may be nothing more than our desperate attempt to legitimate the existing order because it is what we have always known, it is what defines our identity and clarifies our boundaries.

If we as religious people have a particular need for such definition, for coherence and meaning and significance, we should beware. Religious tradition so easily lapses into religious intolerance: history testifies throughout the ages to the havoc wreaked in the name of religion. Is the evasiveness, the transcendence, the otherness of the God of the gospels too much for us to bear? Yet it is only in such a God – far beyond our safe systems and neat demarcations – that salvation lies. And if those on the margins can challenge our complacent beliefs that we know God's thoughts, if they can rampage into the centre of the institution's holy spaces and dismantle our idols, then perhaps there is hope for the Church to be more than a self-perpetuating institution, but a company of people who are together determined to hear the voice of God anew in every generation.

Yet it is part of the scheme of things that human institutions are imperfect. Jettisoning what we have simply leaves a vacuum for something else that will probably in the long run be no better. Many of the images for the coming of the kingdom of God used by Jesus in the gospels suggest gradual transformation: the leaven, the mustard seed, the grain of wheat. The rhythm of death and new birth, the repeated pattern of disillusion and transformation, of the new vitality gradually dying and ossifying and again the crying out for a new start is all a part of the deep structure of the gospel as lived before God's reign has been fully realised. Within this pattern, those at the margins must challenge that which has become complacent or static at the centre. The contemplative ones, the women, those who are homosexual or black or unemployed. They all have a special opportunity, a strategic perspective from which to make space for a new vision of God.

Those in the centre should be careful to listen, to make room, to hear the Word of God challenging the particular idols of our day. Doubtless, new idolatries will in time be forged – the marginalised who have moved to the centre will forget the ambiguity of their erstwhile perspective and new groups will protest from the sidelines. But this is the tendency of our human nature. Yet through all this, the grace of God works silently, patiently, hidden from sight. And the good news of the Christian gospel is that ultimately it will prevail and a reign of love and liberty and justice will be established for ever.

A friend of mine, recently ordained priest, has a poster on her wall which always makes me chuckle. It's a cartoon of two little girls sitting on a bench, pigtails dangling, legs swinging, musing about their future. One of them says: 'When I grow up, I don't know whether I want to be an actress or a bishop.' Maybe, in twenty years' time, people will be wondering what's the joke? Maybe, just maybe, by the grace of God, the notion of women bishops is not unthinkable.

8

The ministry of parish clergy
Michael Wilcock

Michael Wilcock is Vicar of St Nicholas, Durham, previously
having served on the staff of Trinity Theological College, Bristol,
and in a number of other parish appointments.

It was a childhood assumption of my Anglican background,
the background against which I grew up, that in fact 'the
ministry' *was* the parish ministry. To go 'into the ministry'
meant to become a vicar – or a curate (the same thing at an
earlier stage) or a rector (the same thing with a different name).
To be 'in the ministry' meant to be a clergyman working in a
parish.

As time went by, it was borne in upon me that there
was much more to 'the ministry' than that. Parish ministry
operated within a framework not only of parishes but of
deaneries and dioceses, with a substructure of what would in
due course become synodical government, and with personnel
who included bishops, archdeacons, provosts, chaplains, and
many other such dignitaries. Even within the parish, it turned
out that the practice of 'ministry' by people in dog collars was
but the tip of an iceberg, the bulk of which consisted of vast
amounts of ministry carried on by lay people. Then parallel
to this Anglican ministry, lay and clerical, proceeded the ministries of a dozen other denominations; while within it there
would soon emerge new kinds of ordained ministry, with dog
collars now adorning the necks even of ministers who were not
paid, and eventually even of ministers who were not male.

In this connection, therefore, the challenge to 'think
unthinkable' means the challenging of that early, sim-
plistic, traditional assumption, that the parish clergy and

their work *are* 'the ministry'. The reality is so much more complex than anything that could have been comprehended within the limited view of an Anglican child.

I grew up with another set of assumptions. My background was not only an Anglican one, but an evangelical one. I took it for granted that 'what the Bible says' foreclosed all argument. 'What the Bible says' about the Church, therefore, and about the ministry of the Church, was – like what the Bible says about anything else – the last word on the subject, and it could presumably be taken as a blueprint for the Church and the ministry in all subsequent ages.

As time went by, it naturally became evident to me that times had changed, and that the modern world was very different from the world of the Bible. The centuries between had brought all kinds of changes, the sociological and techno-logical ones being only the most obvious of many. In their complexity and sophistication the closing decades of the twen-tieth century seemed light years away from the age in which the Christian Church was established.

So 'thinking the unthinkable' means challenging this second type of assumption too – namely the idea that you can simply lift out of the New Testament its patterns of church life and ministry (always provided, indeed, that you can find any) and transplant them into the Church of today. The unsophisticated gardener might have assumed that this plant would grow anywhere, but a soil and a climate could be so alien as to make him question the assumption.

But now let us embark on a flight of fancy. Let us sup-pose some other unthinkable things. Suppose for example that sauce for the goose really were sauce for the gander? For we ought to apply the questioning of assumptions even-handedly across the board. See how the supposition would relate to these Church situations.

When we compare the Church of England as it is in our day with the churches of the New Testament, and when we compare the world of the late twentieth century with the world of the Bible, it is perfectly obvious that in many respects they are remote from each other and very different. We seem to be comparing the modern and the ancient, the developed and the embryonic, the complex and the simple. So naturally it is the ancient and unsophisticated, the assumptions of childhood, the things we used to take for granted, which have to be questioned. The modern, the sophisticated, are 'reality'; we do not question *them*. But suppose we were to do so? Suppose we were to ask whether the way things are might itself have become a tradition encrusted with assumptions? If it is proper to think the unthinkable about the old simplicities, it must be equally proper to think the unthinkable about the new complexities. Sauce for the goose is sauce for the gander.

Take a couple of instances. Synodical government does its best to bring the Church of England into the twentieth century by replacing its old autocratic structures with new democratic ones. 'Old' in this case is a boo word. On the other hand, the Church's current financial crisis seems to require a strong action from the centre, and so a revival of the old autocracies. 'Old' in this case is a hurrah word. The concept of the monarchical bishop is a time-honoured one, which goes back, if not to the first century, at any rate to the second.

Here are two realities of today's Church which (for two opposite reasons) are seldom questioned. But is either of them, democratisation or centralisation, self-evidently right? Suppose we were to take neither of them, nor indeed a dozen other such realities, for granted?

Here is another unthinkable thing. Suppose the child really were father of the man? For we have to recognise the two different ways in which the primitive Church has developed into the modern Church – what has grown from within, and what has been added from without. The things that really matter were already there in miniature, in principle, when the adult was a child; the rest were not. My bones and my brains belong to me in one sense, my shirts and my shoes in quite another. I may be told that 'That outfit is *you* to a T', but it is not *me* in the same way that my body is *me*. In other words, in this discussion of the Church and its ministry,

I am first forestalling the objection that 'You can't pretend that nineteen centuries of Church history have not happened.' Such an objection begs the question. It is too simple. Are we talking about a continuity of real physical growth, or a mere succession of shirts? I do not ignore the development of the body, but I am quite prepared to ignore the vagaries of fashion. It is easy enough to be caught up with the fascinating topic of what, so to speak, the modern Church is wearing. To that question the nappies of its infancy are irrelevant. But 'the body is more than raiment'. We are concerned with the Church itself, not its clothes. The things that really matter to its adult body we shall surely find, in embryo, in the infant Church. The child is father of the man.

Suppose, then, we were to imagine an ecclesiastical world in which all the traditional structures had been blown away – all the administrations, the hierarchies, the titles, the buildings, the investments were as if they had never been. A hopelessly unrealistic exercise! A ludicrous over-simplification! But suppose, just for the sake of argument, that it were so. Suppose we were to count all these things as merely the clothing of the body rather than as organic parts of it. What would such a stripped-down Church look like?

In that imaginary world the word 'church' would never be used to mean a building, or a denomination, or the bench of bishops, or the ordained ministry. It would mean *the people of God*: nothing more, nothing less. Wherever a group of men and women and boys and girls met in the name of Christ, there would be the Church. They would be there for an encounter with their God as living and as real as their meeting with one another. The power of Word and Spirit would be there, since only by them could such a gathering have come into being, and the ministry of Word and sacrament would be there too, since only by them could it survive.

As well as a local congregation of this kind, the Church would also mean at least the aggregate of all such groups across the face of the earth: all the millions who at any given time come to God through Christ, whatever their language or race or culture.

Vast though such a vision would be, it would still be inadequate. For the term 'universal Church' could not be restricted to God's people now living. It would be seen to denote the far greater company which includes not only these but also their forebears, God's people in all previous generations of the Christian Church – 'upon another shore, and in a greater light, that multitude which no man can number, whose hope was in the Word made flesh, and with whom in the Lord Jesus we are one forever more'. As Hebrews 12:22–24 makes plain, all Christians past and present are actually congregating together around the throne of God in the 'heavenly Jerusalem'.

So this 'stripped-down' version of the Church would be not something lesser, but something greater, than the complexities and pomp of any presently existing denomination, or even of all the modern 'churches' put together. And indeed for a proper description of this Church that we are trying to imagine, even the concept of 'all Christians past as well as present' would not be adequate. For those verses in Hebrews 12 are the climax of a long passage, two chapters whose object is to show that the people of God include all who follow the faith of Abraham in Old Testament as well as New Testament times. As the author says, they, the pre-Christian saints, would not be complete without us, but neither could we be complete without them.

And the Church as the people of God would be greater yet: for the 'Mount Zion' of Hebrews 12, the 'heavenly places' of Ephesians, the 'throne of God' in Revelation 7, that meeting place where the numberless multitudes of his people congregate around him, is a reality outside time, and the saints of future ages are there too. It is a real, actual gathering of God with all his people; and that, be it said, is the true meaning of 'church' – *ekklesia* – throughout Scripture.

In the course of history many of the developments in the life and ministry of the Church have come to seem indispensable, and the loss of them to seem unthinkable. But supposing they *were* lost, stripped off and blown away, two great things would yet remain, because they have been organically part of the body since its birth, not subsequently acquired as part of its wardrobe. (I am speaking now of the people of God in our half of history, the Christian as distinct from the pre-Christian Church, since these things are the promise to which Old Testament believers looked forward, and which was fulfilled in time only with the coming of Christ.) The Christian Church, the Church of our New Testament days, has one great privilege and one great responsibility. These are the two things.

We should not for a moment think of the 'stripping' as being the loss of practically everything that matters, so that we are left with only these as two meagre remnants of the Church's original glory. On the contrary, the 'stripping' would simply serve to enhance this privilege and this responsibility as being themselves the Church's true glory.

In this vision of the Church, what would be its great privilege? It would be a priestly Church. It would have direct access into the presence of God, which is the essence of priesthood. There could be no greater privilege than that. What is more, every member of it would have this privilege. It would be plainly seen that the representative priesthood of the Old Testament had come to an end. In the old days access to God had been restricted to an élite within the people of God, priests who would enter his presence on behalf of the rest. But Christ had taken up and fulfilled that priesthood, opening the way into his Father's presence once and for all: not only at one time for all times, but at one time for all his people. They would thenceforth form, every last one of them, a royal priesthood – a kingdom of priests.

In view of this, it would be seen at once that among the historical trappings that had been blown away must have gone the notion of a priestly élite. It had a place in the Old Testament economy, but only as a pattern which was to be fulfilled in Christ. It was in no way to be reinstated in the New Testament Church, for in that new economy every member would have received from Christ the privileges of his priesthood.

And it would likewise be seen – at last, by a roundabout route, we are approaching 'the ministry of the parish clergy'! – it would be seen that whatever an ordained clergyman is, he is not that. If he *is* a 'priest', he is not a priest in that Old Testament sense, coming to God on behalf of others in a way that they cannot come to God themselves. If he *is* a representative, he is not a representative in that sense. If he *is* 'set apart' for a certain ministry, it is not for that ministry.

Thus the Church's great privilege would be clearly seen, namely that the people of God is a kingdom of priests. What, alongside this, would be its great responsibility?

It would be a prophetic Church. Having been enabled to come *to* God, it would then be sent out *from* God to speak to the world, by life and by lip, on his behalf. As there could be no greater privilege than that of priesthood, so there could be no greater responsibility than this prophetic ministry.

In its broad sense, this too would belong to all the people of God, and not simply to an élite chosen from among them. In the days when God was speaking through his first great prophet Moses, Joshua was disconcerted by the prophesying of two other men, and received the famous reply, 'Would that all the Lord's people were prophets!' Moses' hope came true on the day of Pentecost, when the Spirit was poured out on all flesh; and whatever our stripped-down Church might be deprived of, it would still enjoy that universal prophetic empowering.

The New Testament counterpart of God's prophetic word through Moses at Mount Sinai is the giving of the new law through Christ in his 'sermon' on another mount. In that prophetic word of Christ the prophetic ministry of his Church is spelt out in terms of the functions of salt and light: 'You are the salt of the earth', 'You are the light of the world'.

It would be plain that the Church, and every member of the Church, would have the responsibility of being salt. For all its addiction to spicy fare, ours is a tasteless world. More importantly, for all its pretensions to immortality and its longings for wholeness and permanence, it is a decaying world.

One of the Church's functions is to bring out the flavour of what is good in it, and to inhibit the decay of what is bad in it. In the Church as I am imagining it, every member would be committed to this 'salt' ministry. Every member would be committed to the championing of standards of truth and integrity, of love and care – 'the punishment of wickedness and vice, and the maintenance of thy true religion, and virtue'. Every member would be committed to speaking out on such matters, for speaking out is what prophecy means.

Even more important, because it holds 'promise for both the present life and the life to come', is the responsibility of being light. Within the Church's dual prophetic role, this is the function which looks beyond the end of our age. However assiduously the Church may apply its salt to a tasteless, decaying world, that world will one day perish. After that, what will matter will be how the Church brought its light into a dark world while that world still existed.

The New Testament metaphor of light regularly means the glorious good news of Christ. In my imagined Church, every member would be committed to this 'light' ministry. Every member would be committed to bringing into the dark places around him the message of the forgiveness of sins, and of the gift of a new life over which death has no power, and which 'frees us from all ills, in this world and the next'.

Furthermore, every member would be committed also to being both salt and light in a world which is real, not theoretical. Here again our underlying theme of 'the ministry of the parish clergy' is emerging, for this point exposes both the strength and the weakness of the whole 'parish' concept. It is easy to talk about 'the world' into which the Church is sent as a grandiose theatre of operations somewhere out there, and to evolve plans for the Church's witness in the world as an enterprise to be carried on in exotic distant places by people whom we will depute to do it, supported of course by our prayers and gifts, but supported from afar. It is equally easy, in doing so, to overlook the challenge to prophetic witness which is right under our noses. The parish system is one way of ensuring that we face the nearer challenge as well as the remoter one. Every local church must be committed to the community in which its members live. Here the theory of worldwide mission is earthed in reality.

On the other hand, the parish system in its English form is nowadays only a limited part of that reality. In England 'parishioners' means 'everyone who resides within the parish boundary' (the word does not necessarily mean this elsewhere), and the community of people who happen to live in the same locality is by no means the only kind of community the Church has to recognise today. The residents in an Anglican parish may still be the spiritual responsibility of the local Anglican church, but most of them do not 'belong' to that church in any other sense. Education, work, leisure, and facility of travel, all create new kinds of community, which keep people constantly crossing (and ignoring) parish boundaries.

So my imagined Church, the people of God all committed to their prophetic responsibility, would be addressing *every* community to which it related in any realistic way. It would be investing prayer and energy, manpower and money, in growth points near and far. Conversely, it would be prepared to sit very loose to modes of prophetic witness which had outlived their usefulness.

So far, then, the Church of my fantasy, having been deprived of so much of its traditional garb, is reduced to being simply the people of God, all of whose members – of the generation, that is, at present living on this earth – have the privilege of being priests and the responsibility of being prophets.

And is that all? That, I should have thought, is practically enough! To any who might protest, and say of such a ruthlessly simplified portrait of the Church what Mark Anthony said of the murdered Caesar ('Are all thy conquests, glories, triumphs, spoils, shrunk to this little measure?'), I should retort that he had not grasped the greatness of the thing portrayed.

But even so it is not quite enough, not quite all. For the question would remain as to how the Church would be equipped for its far-reaching responsibilities. On the pattern of the priesthood of ancient Israel, God would have washed all his people in the blood of Christ and clothed them all in the righteousness of Christ in order that they, all of them, should have free priestly access to him. He would have done this once and for all on the day when he made them his own. As they were then turned around, so to speak, in order to go out *from* him, how would he fit them for an effective prophetic ministry to the world?

This also he could no doubt do instantly and miraculously. But in fact he would choose otherwise. Where the Church was an effective instrument in his hands, truly the salt of the earth and the light of the world, it would be because of those within it whom he had chosen for the task of making it so, progressively and not instantaneously. These would have the function of teaching and training it, rebuking and encouraging it, feeding and guarding and guiding it, and thus equipping it to be what he wanted it to be. It would be through their ministry that God by his Spirit would forge his instrument, a Church which would embody the gospel and bring Christ to the world.

That is what I think the Church might look like if some unthinkable gale were to blow away the time-honoured trappings of nineteen centuries, and leave it in an unthinkable nakedness. But the conjuring up of a picture of such absurd naiveté gives me an odd sense of *déjà vu*. And then I realise where I have seen it before. It is remarkably like the picture of those unsophisticated Churches of the New Testament. You go back beyond the last nineteen centuries, back to the first of the twenty, and you find that this is what the original simplicities were. You find a Church which is simply the people of God, either as groups of them meet physically in this or that particular place, or as all of them meet spiritually around the throne of God. You find them all enjoying the prerogative of priests in their direct access to God through the once-for-all priesthood of Christ. You find them all taking on the task of prophets, holding forth the word of life in the midst of a crooked and perverse generation. And you find them led and guided in this life and ministry by 'shepherds', who are

MINISTRY

mature Christians, chosen to oversee them (*pastors* who are
presbyters, and who *bishop*!). Nor are these leaders an élite:
there is no élitism in this Church; just as all God's people
are priests and prophets, so all are ministers, each with gifts
for the upbuilding of the Church. All have vocations, and all
have been ordained by God to some function, and being a
pastor/presbyter/bishop is simply one function among many.

I am describing the Church as I see it in the pages of the New
Testament. But why should I not be describing the Church as it
is today? Is there any reason why this simple outline should not
suffice for the present-day life and ministry of God's people?

It is worth laying the new against the old to see how the
two outlines compare. Some features tally in both shape and
name: you could describe what happens today in terms taken
directly from the New Testament. Some features have changed
their names, but the shapes tally. We know 'ministers'
whose work is that of a Philippian 'bishop', and 'bishops'
who are doing what Acts 6 would call 'ministering at
tables'. Some features are para-church structures, structures
which have grown up alongside the Church, to facilitate its
work and witness: missionary societies, publishing houses,
charities and trusts. All such things can readily be justified as relating directly to the organic life of the body.

On the other hand, there are things which have become well
established features of church life, often over many years or
even centuries, without in fact having any clear or necessary
relation to the fundamental pattern I have been speaking of.
It is these that the unthinkable wind would blow away. In a
time of ease the Church may carry them without realising that
its work is hindered rather than helped by them. But in a time
of crisis we cannot afford this.

The ministry of the parish clergy is in outline a shape which
tallies, or should tally, remarkably closely with the ministry
of shepherds/presbyters/bishops within a local church as the
New Testament describes it. I see no conceivable situation in
which the Church of Christ can ever do without such a ministry.
More specialised ministries, more sophisticated structures, on

the other hand, may come and go. Their viability or otherwise is determined by the question, 'Do they foster, or do they inhibit, the work and witness of the actual grass-roots churches in their actual local communities?'

I supposed earlier in this chapter the blowing away of all the administrations, hierarchies, titles, buildings, investments. Should I be glad to see such a cataclysm? That would depend. I magnify my office, as the Apostle Paul said. I see the work of the parish clergy as being absolutely central to the life of the Church. It is an essential feature – one of the few essential features – of a Church which perpetuates the dynamic New Testament pattern. It is the pastor enabling the congregation in the work of the gospel. That being so, I have a lot of time for a structure like an Anglican diocese, with its bishops and offices and accountants and advisers, when it recognises its function as a para-church structure – when it directs its efforts to enabling the pastors to enable the congregations.

Conversely, I have no time for it when it doesn't. Make it do what it is meant to do; if it won't, by all means blow it away. For the world is real people, and the world needs the salt and light of the Church, which is also real people in real contact with it; and the Church needs the shepherding of its parish clergy, who are likewise real people in real living personal relationships with it. That is the 'coal face' of ministry. There is no other Christian service quite like it. If the Lord calls you to be a dignitary or an academic or a committee person or an ecclesiastical politician, well, good for you: may he make up to you what you are missing!

The ministry of bishops

Ruth Etchells

Ruth Etchells was the first lay Principal of St John's College, Durham, and is a present member of the Crown Appointments Commission.

In 1990, Church House Publishing produced the weighty *Report of the Archbishops' Group on the Episcopate*,[1] the end product of four years' intensive and often bitter debate in a group which in itself represented not only the deep divisions within the Church of England about the ordination of women to the priesthood, but also the profounder polarities which exist within the Church. For, as the Bishop of Ely once argued in a former professional manifestation, our present Anglican doctrine of the Church is a paradoxical one (he used the word 'incoherent') since incorporated into its basic documents is the internal contradiction between Protestant Reformation principles of 'things necessary to salvation', which did not include episcopacy though it allowed it; and Catholic principles and perceptions re-established at the Restoration, which required it. The episcopate, its nature and function, is at the heart of this mixed inherited tradition of our Church. And yet I want to suggest that, for that very reason, it can be a sign of the unity which holds these polarities together.

Five years on, inter-church ecumenical dialogue has helped us also in this internal dialogue, as, for instance, the Anglican-Lutheran Porvoo Statement, to which I shall return later, demonstrates. We have begun to move away from such issues as mechanistic physical questions of 'apostolic succession', and even from too rigid a definition of 'episcopacy' itself, to a recognition that 'episcope', 'oversight', is to be found and honoured in more than one form. Acknowledging it as something necessary and common to all Christian communities, I want us to reflect on its present form in the Church of England, what that is meant to embody, and how it does or does not do that.

For when we talk about 'episcope', oversight, and our particular form of it in the Church of England, we are not just talking about organisation and structures: we are talking about what kind of a community we as the Church understand ourselves to be, baptised in the faith of salvation through Christ, in the name of the Father, Son and Holy Spirit. We are a people of the Word, nourished and rooted in the Scriptures, as we affirm in the 39 Articles. We are also a people bonded by God's gift of the sacrament of the Eucharist, gathered at Christ's table. And both our sacramental life and our life in the scriptural Word flow from our corporate and individual living relationship with the triune God, Father, Son, and Holy Spirit. That is, we are a trinitarian people and our understanding of our life together, including how we think of the oversight of our leaders, must be understood in that context.

It was, in fact, the experience of the reality and power of that trinitarian theology which enabled that deeply divided working group to produce its volume on the episcopate; for we found alive and at work among us two complementary experiences of the triune God, and in their interaction we were able to hold together in division. Specifically, in their interaction we began to see how to hold together not only the emphasis on Word of some, and on sacrament of others, but the differences between us concerning forms of 'headship', and the tensions between us concerning the 'sacramental' or 'functional' reality of episcopacy.

The dominant trinitarian theology in the Report was to prove to be that known as 'subordinationist': that is, of the ordered relationship of Father, Son and Spirit with God the Father as sovereign, the sole source of authority and initiative. Many in the Church would today challenge the model of episcopacy that seems to follow, with its emphasis on a 'headship' authoritative rather than co-operative, unitary rather than plural, hierarchical rather than mutual.

But another trinitarian theology was present in that Report also, that of the inter-dependence of Father, Son and Spirit, so perfect in mutality that they will one will. This points to a very different kind of headship, one of mutual giving and receiving, of collaboration as a way of being as well as doing. The truth is, of course, that neither theology would be complete without the other: each safeguards a necessary truth of divine authority, one of hierarchy, one of mutuality. And this complementarity inherent in our Anglican trinitarian theology, this safeguarding of necessary truths, can be brought to bear on the way we think about our episcopate.

Take, for instance, the issue with which I was initially faced when I was asked to write this chapter. The title I was given was: 'The ministry of bishops' – or, 'Elected for a fixed term?' In other words, was being a bishop a 'job' you picked up for a time and then put down, or was it of a different nature? Though the current formularies make the present official view of the Church of England quite clear, there is certainly among us a strong and articulate group, particularly among evangelicals, who would hold that, properly, episcopacy should be seen as the former – a 'job', a role, which should not be held for longer than a certain period. I cannot myself (though an evangelical) take this view, and I hope what follows will help to explain why.

In a sense, of course, bishops in the Church of England are actually elected for a fixed term: it happens to be the rest of their lives, barring whatever unthinkable sin would require de-consecrating a bishop. Pleasing speculation though this be, it is the solid fact behind it we need to tackle. Bishops in the Church of England are *consecrated* as bishops, not commissioned or admitted or installed but *consecrated*: and so the process which makes them bishops is understood to affect their state of being, not just their function. This is the sacramental understanding of what happens at the consecration service: their function follows from the gift of grace, not the other way round. It is the same kind of Anglican understanding as that of ordination, which insists that once you are ordained priest you are priest for the fixed term of the rest of your life, whatever 'job' you go on to do, inside or outside the Church. This is neither a mechanistic nor a magical view of either ordination or of consecration: it is simply giving full weight to the words of the Ordinal, and what is manifestly both their intention and expectation. A special gift of grace is prayed for, appropriate to this person in this order of calling.

So the key issue, when we are thinking of whether it would be a 'better thing' to have ten-year bishops who then revert simply to the order of priesthood again, is whether we wish to put the primary emphasis on the jobs/tasks to be done, functions to be fulfilled in the context of certain management levels; or whether we are thinking of God raising up for himself men – and women too, before too long, here as well as elsewhere – for a particular kind of leadership which is focused in what he makes of them, through a special kind of grace, for all that is inherent in sharing in the corporate leadership of the whole Church.

And right away the problem is clear. The first kind of language I was using was that of straight 'line-management', role and task analysis: which, as the Church's critics rightly point out, seems sadly lacking in the Church. It is the language of efficient secular organisation. The second kind of language has in it some terms meaningless in the secular world: 'God raising up for himself leaders': why not translate this as the organisation spotting the leaders it needs for particular roles and tasks, from its own members, and developing a process to bring them on and appoint them. Or, 'leadership focused in what God makes of them through a particular kind of grace' – has that any meaning at all, the secular world asks (and so do some in the Church) other than that if the Church has spotted right, then these people have the capacity to grow in the task: possibly beyond the task, and so become Archbishops, no less.

Of course it is quite clear that the secular world is right in insisting on, as essential, a process by which the Church as an organisation identifies and develops its natural leaders: but always with the caveat that, as the history of God's people has proved, God's calling to leadership has begged the question from time to time about what we may rightly discern as 'natural' in leadership in such a context as this. But, with that caveat, yes, the Church has the responsibility to be constantly discerning and encouraging its natural leaders, and indeed they must have the capacity to grow on the job. However it would be quite wrong for either the secular world or the 'short term appointment party' within the Church to dismiss the rest as a sort of mystical/ecclesiastical mumbo-jumbo, a jargon that Church of England hierarchies fall into whenever they want to create a defensive smoke-screen of mystery. For the element that the secular world leaves out of discussion about line-management in the Church is the term 'God'. And since the Church is about God and for God and upheld by God and has no purpose other than God, God has to be the prime element, at the centre, when you are talking about the leadership of his people. *Really* the prime element, not just a matter of lip-service; which is why seriously seeking his will has to be built in formally to the process of electing bishops, as carefully as all the human issues of management selection. Built in, too, to what is looked for in their 'oversight' when they have been elected.

And here, it seems to me, we have a first glimpse of how the complementarity of our Protestant and Catholic inheritance in the Church of England can be seen at work in our version of episcope. For if the emphasis is, in the consecration, sacramental, and therefore often felt to be primarily Catholic in its understanding, the earliest and still primary focus of that special grace given was and is

> to ensure the authoritativeness of the transmission of the message to new generations of Christians. . . . Irenaus wrote of the bishop as a minister of unity in this sense

– as the one who keeps the local church in the apostolic teaching . . . a tradition open and public, based on the Scriptures . . . outward continuity in the consecration of bishops in succession was here a sign of inward continuity of teaching. . . . So it was the bishop's responsibility to unfold the Scriptures to the people at the Sunday Eucharist, so as to bring the Bible to bear on the events of daily life, and to help the people grow in understanding and knowledge of the faith.[2]

Such an understanding brings together the Catholic emphasis on sacramental continuity, and the Protestant emphasis on the bishop's rootedness in Scripture, in a rich way.

So am I suggesting that those Churches which view this differently, and have moderators or superintendents appointed for seven or ten years, do not 'seek out the will of God' in relation to their leadership as seriously as the Church of England does? No, I'm not suggesting that. I speak as a former Congregationalist myself, well persuaded of the holiness and true calling of the ministry of such Churches, among whom was numbered my own father. And yet, paradoxically, it was partly the richness and depth of the Church of England's understanding of its leadership as an episcopate which drew me away from Congregationalism and into Anglicanism.

Let us look further into this understanding. Very recently the British and the Irish Anglican Churches came together with all the Nordic and Baltic Lutheran Churches – across Lithuania, Latvia, Estonia, Finland, Sweden, Norway, Denmark, Iceland and Greenland, to make a common declaration called 'The Porvoo Common Statement',[3] and to become interchangeably in communion with each other – a piece of major and wonderful ecumenism about which flags should be flying. One of the major issues which had formerly divided these Churches and now united them was the issue of 'bishops'. So they had to sit down together and work out what was their fundamental common belief about bishops, what they were and what they were for. From this has come therefore, a truly contemporary statement about episcope as the Church of England understands it, one which was recently formally endorsed by the Church of England's General Synod.[4]

What the Statement declared was that the episcopal office was to be retained 'as a sign of our intention under God, to ensure the continuity of the Church in apostolic life and witness'.[5] 'Continuity' in the life of the Church, continuity with, unity with, that first Apostolic Church, was the key. It is the Church itself, the whole Church, which in every age declares itself to be 'apostolic' – at one with, continuous with, in unity with, that first apostolic Church: as we affirm in our Creed: 'We believe in one holy, catholic and apostolic Church'.

Such a Church, the statement affirms, has certain permanent characteristics which must be present if it is to be thus continuous with its past. It must witness to the same faith as the Apostles; it must proclaim and freshly interpret the gospel; it must celebrate baptism and the Eucharist; it must effect the transmission of ministerial responsibilities from one generation to the next; it must seek to be united in prayer, love, joy and suffering, in service to the sick and needy; it must promote unity among the local churches and share the gifts which God has given to each.[6]

These are the permanent features of the Church through the ages; and in every age God pours out his gifts and raises up men and women to sustain such a Church – an apostolic Church – to his glory. Within such a Church the ordained ministry is also a continuity which focuses the continuity of the whole through its ministry and helps to unite it. Its continuity is emphasised (not effected) by the 'laying on of hands' which reminds the Church that it receives its mission from Christ himself.

Every Church finds the necessity for some kind of episcope, oversight, of such ministry: a caring for the whole life of the Christian community, including pastoring the pastors. The Church of England version of such episcope, its episcopacy, is that such oversight must never be in isolation: and it is in this that it most clearly reflects that understanding of the

Trinity as divine mutuality, of which I spoke earlier. For just as the whole Church must reflect, grow from, the nature of the triune God in whom it lives, so must its parts, and most particularly its leadership.

So the episcopacy must not be isolated in time, but connected through its continuity. And it must cross space, which it does by its collegiate nature, since every bishop is, in his diocese, collegial with his diocese (usually through his Synod); moreover he carries this with him into his collegial relationship with all his fellow-bishops of the Church of England, and beyond that with all his fellow-bishops of the worldwide Anglican Church. And beyond that with all the fellow-bishops of the different Churches with whom we are at last moving into fuller communion. Such an episcopacy is also, as well as *collegiate, communal*, because no bishop in the Church of England can be appointed to other than an area, a local community; and his duty is to work within that community to tell out the good news of God's love in Christ, to offer Christian leadership, to serve God, and to be a centre of unity in him for that community.

And yet that oversight, while never isolated, is personal: because at the laying on of hands, at the moment of consecration, the whole Church represented by those present calls upon God to pour out the Holy Spirit in a special gift of grace, not on the task to be done, but on the one being consecrated. If the words of the prayers said then mean anything at all, that is what they mean. And in so consecrating, the Church today is doing what the Apostles did, and what the Church through the ages has done. And the Apostles didn't do it for a ten-year stint, but for life! I find myself pondering on the Apostle Paul's probable reaction to a suggestion that the Apostles' successors should only endure for ten years the intense pressure of the task, and then be pulled out of such hardship. I think his language would have been both vehement and picturesque! And I muse on Bishop Polycarp of the early Church, aged eighty, enduring the forced march to Rome so that he could, with his people with whom he was by consecration united, suffer death by wild beast in the Colosseum, as the right outliving of his episcopacy in its witness to faith.

So it is the apostolic nature of the role, so clearly attested by Scripture and by the Church's life through the ages, which for me makes episcopacy as a short-term 'appointment' a contradiction in terms. And this emphasis on continuity is not about 'safeguarding' in the sense of 'monumentalising' how the Church does things, but about acknowledging God's faithfulness to his Church. It is about men in this kind of ultimate leadership, living out their lives, whatever comes for the rest of their natural span, in faithfulness to that calling and the personal grace given for it. Such seem to me to speak of the faithfulness of God, who doesn't himself work to a ten-year span either.

Am I therefore arguing that all is perfect with our episcopate in the Church of England? No, emphatically not: but before I could look at how we may amend, it seemed to me essential to affirm the essential nature of our Church's episcopate as properly scriptural, rooted in a trinitarian theology which acknowledges both hierarchy and mutuality as true to the Church's life, and drawing in its strengths on both the Catholic and Protestant traditions of our Church. How we appoint our bishops, and what we do with them when we've got them: that's another issue altogether, and to that I now briefly turn.

How are (diocesan) bishops appointed? I speak as a long serving member of the Crown Appointments Commission, charged with that task. When a see is announced as falling vacant, a 'Vacancy in See Committee' is called together in the diocese, one which includes most of its clerical and lay leaders. They draw up a 'Statement of Diocesan Needs', which will be put before the Crown Appointments Commission. They also elect four of their number to become fully part of the Crown Appointments Commission for the meeting concerning their diocese. They also meet with the two Appointments Secretaries – the Prime Minister's and the Archbishops': and these two emissaries also meet with a hundred or more representatives of the diocese, such as county councillors, education leaders, business leaders, industrialists, social services, and leaders of the other Churches and other faiths in the area. They produce their own Report on the Needs of the Diocese as they have observed them. This Report is circulated with the other one to the Crown Appointments Commission, including its four diocesan members.

Then the Crown Appointments Commission meets. It consists of the two Archbishops, six members elected from General Synod (three lay, three clergy) plus the four diocesan members; with in attendance the Prime Minister's and Archbishops' Appointments Secretaries. We always meet in secrecy, so that the media can't lobby us; and in a House of Prayer, so that there's continuing prayer going on all the time.

In the period between the announcement of the vacancy and the meeting, names have been suggested to the Crown Appointments Commission members who can forward them with their own ideas; and the diocese also may suggest names. These make up a long list, perhaps up to ten or twelve. Our task at our residential meeting is, by listening and praying, to reduce those names to two, either of whom we are clear could be God's bishop for that particular diocese . . . that particular diocese. A name splendid for one would be quite wrong for another: the fact that, as we noted earlier, the bishop is bishop *to a locality* is vital. We listen to the diocesan members and we study all the material gathered, very thoroughly and painstakingly. And finally we vote. Both names must have 75 per cent support before they can go forward. And that is how the Church – the Church, not the Prime Minister – chooses its bishops. The Prime Minister's role is limited to choosing between those two names, though he has the right to refuse them and ask for two more, a right I can't remember ever being exercised.

Now, secularly speaking, there are a lot of questions. No interviews? How good is the information gathered, particularly about those being named? How effective is the process of bringing forward names? I'm quite certain all that could be improved, though it's actually already of a remarkably high standard. On the other hand, the whole exercise is quite literally centred upon an expectation that the Holy Spirit will, as a reality, be present guiding our discussion. Of course human self-will and intransigence can get in the way. But when we get stuck, we stop and pray. When we get frustrated, we stop and pray. We say the Offices together. We sleep on it, having said our prayers. We receive Holy Communion together, in the morning. And then we decide. God truly is at the centre.

What, then, do I argue most needs reform? Why, the misunderstanding within the Church of England which could frame such a notion of episcopacy as potentially fixed-term, since it makes line-management – 'oversight' in the administrative sense – the key role, indeed the definition, of bishophood. But the bishop's 'oversight' is of his people's whole being with the whole of his being, particularly their stages of pilgrimage heavenwards, a journey he must, like Polycarp, make with them. He is there to resource them in that, and to pastor their pastors in that; and to be such takes a grace endowment of the whole person. He is not a business administrator, yet he must ensure his diocese is kept out of debt; he is not a managing director, yet he must harness his work teams effectively for God; he is not a social worker, yet he must have on his heart the sharp needs of the vulnerable of his locality; he is not a headmaster, yet he must ensure the faith is consistently and profoundly and clearly taught; he is not an entertainer, yet he must give hundreds of public 'performances' a year; he is not necessarily an academic, yet he must be well informed theologically and able to think deeply and clearly himself and challenge others to do so also. He is, often, a member of the House of Lords, a peer, yet he must remain utterly accessible to the humblest. He has a national, public role as a leader of the established Church; yet the Church of England's active worshippers are probably less than three per cent of the population. What he must be, beyond all this, is a man whose life is totally rooted in his love of God, a man of ceaseless and active prayer, of deep pastoral compassion, alight with the good news for the world and growing in God all the time.

So what ought to be changed is the Church's expectation and view of him: which might, in time, affect society's view of him. It is not status or rank that is of the least importance here, as any bishop realises quickly once in office. It is the pastoral authority of the bishop that needs re-emphasising, rediscovering, the fact that he is a leader of a vast voluntary organisation which is both human and divine, endowed by God and living its human life in that endowment to honour God and serve the world.

I chose for the reading from which this chapter grew the Gospel set for the Consecration Service of a bishop: that lovely passage (John 21:15–17) describing Christ's encounter of forgiveness and authorising of Simon Peter, after the resurrection, beside the lake after the simple breakfast of bread and fish. I chose it because it underlines two things. First, that Peter was authorised by Christ in his 'oversight' role after being, humanly speaking, a failure, showing, to put it kindly, cowardice and disloyalty. The people the Church calls, in God's name, to be bishops, are all ordinary folk like Peter, called out to be beyond the ordinary for Christ. Do not ever let us expect of them faultlessness. They come not necessarily because they are saintlier than anyone else (though they may be, or may grow to be) but because God has put his finger on them.

The second thing about this Consecration Gospel is the nature of the calling: 'Feed my sheep; feed my lambs . . .' If as a Church we would rethink our attitude to bishops, and lay aside our deep defensiveness in matters of potential power play, so that we could honour and delight in their gift of pastoral authority, hierarchical and mutually dependent, without fear for our freedoms, then the bishops could be set more free themselves to be truly shepherds, nourishing their people in food for their souls, tending them so that they grow in love and obedience to Christ. Then no one would see much point in arguing for a 'fixed term bishop'.

It was George Lindbeck, in his discussion of these issues in relation to Anglican/Roman Catholic dialogue, who caught for me best what I have been propounding. Speaking of that unity towards which we are under Christ's direct command to strive, he wrote:

> The messianic pilgrim people which is the body of Christ in history needs unifying institutional structures. These structures are to be assessed and reformed functionally by the evangelical touchstone of whether they help the churches witness faithfully by all they are, say and do, to Christ, in the power of the Spirit and to the glory of God the Father. These structures, however, as catholics stress, are also gifts of God to be gratefully received and obediently used to his glory. Episcopacy can be one such gift to the whole church . . .

The ministry of cathedrals

John Arnold

John Arnold is the catholic Dean of Durham

Jesus told this parable to some who trusted in themselves that they were righteous and despised others. Two men went up to the temple to pray, one a Pharisee and the other a tax collector. The Pharisee standing by himself was praying thus, 'God, I thank you that I am not like other people: thieves, rogues, adulterers or even like this tax collector. I fast twice a week, I give a tenth of all my income.' But the tax collector standing far off would not even look up to heaven but was beating his breast and saying, 'God, be merciful to me, a sinner' (Luke 18:9–14).

This is just to set the scene in the temple for what I want to say about cathedrals, which Richard Hooker taught us to regard as temples of the living God: but I take as my text an old Punch cartoon, that splendid full-page du Maurier picture from the first decade of this century, showing a young Edwardian beauty with hour-glass figure reclining upon a chaise longue and receiving a visit from a very proper young curate in full morning dress, his top hat, stick and gloves set out on a stool beside him. He is leaning forward and asking her earnestly: 'My dear, would you rather be beautiful or good?' And she, gazing back at him in sultry fashion through heavy-lidded eyes, is murmuring: 'I would rather be beautiful and repent.'

In cathedrals we have no choice. We can only be beautiful – and repent. I do not need to speak to you of beauty – the stone, the wood, the glass and iron, the flowers, the setting, the music all speak for themselves: and we thank all those living and departed who have contributed to these many delights. It is however worth pausing to note that the very fact that we take the alliance of beauty and worship for granted in cathedrals such as ours has been bought at a great price. If the Empress Irene II, a battleaxe of the first water even by Byzantine standards – if she had not won the iconoclastic controversy with blood and tears, if the Anglicans led by Richard Hooker had not defeated the Puritans in the interpretation of the Elizabethan settlement, if church and king and Bishop Cosin and the Book of Common Prayer had not been restored after the Commonwealth, we would of course still be worshipping God, but in bare buildings with maimed rites and plain notes if any. And, therefore, with a diminished view of Almighty God, Father, free, loving, creative, sovereign, spontaneous and joyful, and of his Son who came to raise our human nature by adoption and grace to the level of his own likeness and of the Holy and life-giving Spirit, through whom the love of God is shed abroad in our hearts. Cathedrals exist to keep open a large view of God and of his goodness and a large view of human potentiality as well as a realistic view of human sinfulness. That is why the two subjects of our sonata are beauty and repentance.

And we have plenty to repent of: we must have, or the General Synod would not have passed the Care of Cathedrals Measure of 1990 with its alarming penalties and insulting implications; and the Archbishops would not have set up a Commission to inquire into all aspects of cathedral life, especially their governance. We must have, or we would not be continually compared disparagingly with parish churches, rather quaintly and indeed acrobatically described as simultaneously the backbone and the front line and the glory of the Church of England. There is only one glory of the Church of England and that is neither its parish churches nor its cathedrals – it is the transmission of the gospel, the scandal of the crucifixion, the preaching of the cross of Christ. It is by that comparison alone, in the light of and at the foot of the cross that we have much – indeed everything – to repent of.

And cathedrals, which offer us so much temptation, like the scribes and Pharisees, to enjoy greetings in the market place and the best seats in the synagogue, also offer us the opportunity simply to follow the publican and go to the temple to pray and give up trying to make ourselves acceptable by our works to God or man, to commissions or committees, to all the people who write in with their complaints – a tiny proportion it is true of those who write appreciatively – but still to be heeded, to give up pretending, to give up trying to justify ourselves and to substitute justification by works for justification by faith and justification by self for justification by God. I answer every letter I receive, painstakingly explaining what we do and why we do it, apologising when we are in the wrong, pushing back when it seems to me that we are in the right. But often because I know that I and my colleagues and the whole system of religion by which we are trammelled are so deeply corrupted by sin, I just want to drop my pen or close my lips, and only open them to say, 'God have mercy on me a sinner.' And then I realise that I cannot even do that, because in cathedrals we pay other people to sing these words for us, hauntingly and agonisingly beautifully, so that the meaning is simultaneously obscured and enhanced, *Kyrie eleison, Christe eleison, Kyrie eleison*.

Cathedrals are places for experiencing deeply the all-embracing corruption of sin and – even more deeply – the all-embracing scope and grandeur of the love of God. A Russian Orthodox priest, drawing heavily on his knowledge of Byzantium, said to me when he learned that I was Dean of an English Cathedral (Rochester then, not Durham): 'Father John, when there is very great beauty there is always very great wickedness.' That is true and one of the reasons why it is true is that some people give themselves to the cult of the beauty of inanimate objects not as a means of enhancing their love of God and neighbour but as a substitute for them.

And that is idolatry. A year after the 400th anniversary of the birth of George Herbert I quote:

> A man that looks on glass
> On it may stay his eye
> Or, if he pleaseth, through it pass
> And there the heaven espy.

It is precisely because of the magnitude of temptation and the certainty of falling that cathedrals which are places of such great wickedness must also be places given over to forgiveness. When Michael Turnbull, now Bishop of Durham, joined us at Rochester as a Canon, after being Archbishop's Chaplain and parish priest and University Chaplain and Chief Secretary of the Church Army, he said to me: 'Now in middle life I have rediscovered grace. Everywhere else I was expected to take the lead, to achieve something, to work wonders. Here I step onto a moving travellator of mattins and evensong; and the faith which I need, I do not have to make for myself. It is the faith of the Church.' Let us hope he rediscovers it here.

Now listen to another voice. 'Lara was not religious . . . she did not believe in ritual' – that's not me, that's Boris Pasternak in his masterpiece *Doctor Zhivago*:

> Lara was not religious . . . she did not believe in ritual; but sometimes, to enable her to bear her life she needed the accompaniment of an inward music and she could not always compose it for herself. The music was God's word of life and it was to weep over it that she went to church. Once at the beginning of December . . . she went to pray with such a heavy heart that she felt as if at any moment the earth might open at her feet and the vaulted ceiling of the church cave in . . . In the time it took her to make her way past the worshippers, buy two candles and find her place, the deacon had rattled off the nine Beatitudes at a pace suggesting that they were quite well enough known without his help. Blessed are the poor in spirit . . . blessed are they that mourn . . . blessed are they that hunger and thirst after righteousness . . .

Lara trembled and stood still. This was for her. He was saying: Happy are the downtrodden. There is after all something to be said for them. They have everything before them. That was what Christ thought. That was his opinion.

That's magical, isn't it? Only a great poet could have written that as the best expression I know in prose of what can happen in cathedrals, where wounded souls can slip in, feeling like death, and hide behind the pillars and listen to someone else singing the liturgy and be touched by God's word of life and be broken down and lifted up in one and the same movement, and know that they count, that they are a child of God, worth far more than any sparrow. Pasternak, who was a great sinner as well as a great poet, not very brave, not very faithful, was preserved by God alone of all the poets of the Russian silver age; he was preserved to write that, to say what God's grace can do for the teenage mistress of a middled-aged roué and he could say it because he knew what it could do for him.

It can do the same for us and for our cathedrals and for all who come to them, seeking beauty which they know they are seeking; and repentance, which they may not know they are seeking until they hear the music or God's word of life, which they cannot compose for themselves – and now at last realise that they do not need to, because both repentance and forgiveness are free gifts, pure grace. For which we, taking the advice of St Paul to the Colossians, should be thankful and let the Word of Christ dwell in us as richly . . . as we sing psalms and hymns and spiritual songs with thankfulness in our hearts to God.

The form in which God's word of life came to Lara was the chanting of the Beatitudes: Blessed are the poor in spirit, blessed are they that mourn, blessed are they that hunger and thirst after righteousness; but it could have come through glass, or painting, through sculpture or embroidery or simply through the building itself.

And I want to insist that it is the cathedral itself – the cathedral in its wholeness and integrity – which is our main concern and something greater than any of its parts or the sum of its parts. I could go on to speak of individual works of art which contribute to the cathedral and which are enhanced by being set in a cathedral, but it is the cathedral itself which is primary and which it is our task to maintain. For cathedrals witness, in an age of fragmentation and specialisation, of analysis rather than synthesis, of division rather than cohesion, to a unity of purpose and a harmony of many different voices which can convey wholeness and healing to a generation which needs these things above all else.

These great buildings by their size and magnanimity and by the regular offering of worship, can give shape to God's two great gifts of space and time for people who in their everyday lives never have enough of either, because they perceive them as formless and of no worth. Cathedrals speak freely of the spaciousness and generosity of God in creation as well as the continuity of the Church and the creativity of men and women through the ages, including our own. This is one reason why entry to cathedrals should, if possible, be free; it should be an experience, not a transaction.

All the English cathedrals now give great care to welcoming visitors and helping them appreciate what they find. It is a fine art to make available sufficient explanatory material while still leaving enough unspoken, so that visitors are given the opportunity to have their own experiences of transcendence, rather than have second-hand experiences thrust upon them. In all that we do, we seek to help tourists become pilgrims, because we know that pilgrimage is a fine and enlarging human experience while tourism can be narrow and alienating. Pilgrimages grew up because of the association of saints and sanctity with particular places; and it has always been a task for the Church to lead pilgrims on from an interest in physical objects to the personal and spiritual associations which they bear.

All the great English medieval shrines were destroyed in 1547; but their sites have remained known and hallowed and they are not only increasingly appreciated today, but are even being added to. Canterbury, for example, the scene of the martyrdom of Thomas Becket now houses in its Corona a notable chapel to the martyrs of the twentieth century. Rochester was the Bishopric both of John Fisher (+ 1535) and of Nicholas Ridley (+ 1555), who died for their faith and for conscience though on different sides at the time of the Reformation. The double cult of these martyrs is an inspiration to us now in the ecumenical perspectives of the late twentieth century. Many people visit Rochester Cathedral, where I used to be Dean, because it is the church which Charles Dickens knew and loved; and other cathedrals have their own literary and secular saints. The continual re-telling of heroic tales and the preservation of the corporate memory of society through annual commemorations is part of the rhythm of cathedral life and a great contribution to the culture of the nation.

Many of us long for the day when once again the Church will be a major patron of the arts; and personalities will be formed by the expression in wood and stone, in bronze and silk, of a truly Christian humanism. For the moment, the financial means just do not lie to hand; and we can only report isolated instances and the attempt of some churchmen, at least, to stay in contact with creative artists and craftsmen. Certainly I can bear witness that the single most satisfying episode in my ministry as Dean of Rochester was the time I spent discussing the incarnation with a sculptor, preparing for us a statue of Mary and the Child Christ, donated by a single generous benefactor and now giving pleasure to many who rejoice to see this representation of a mother and child, and deepening the faith of those who see in them the Son of God and the Mother of God.

What I enjoyed fleetingly at Rochester during a single com-mission, some cathedrals, notably Durham, have enjoyed more permanently by boldly – after the manner of universities with their writers-in-residence – employing an artist-in-residence. The clergy speak of the enrichment and challenge which comes to us and to our modes of perception from having an artist in our midst: and the artists speak of the inspiration which comes from the cathedral, both as a building and as a way of life.

For the greatest contribution cathedrals make to culture is not the patronage or preservation of individual works of art: it is the living of life in a community, open to the world around it and sensitive to its needs, but deriving its rhythms and its values from elsewhere, so that it may continue to offer something new and challenging, healing and refreshing to the world and to the rest of the Church. All the elements which sociologists tell us are necessary for community are there: space, time, folklore, symbols, shared memories and common purposes. These things make possible mutual care, reliable relationships and growth into personal maturity for the poor in spirit and those who mourn. And by making the major concerns of the age their own and conveying them to their dioceses, they can also encourage and succour those who hunger and thirst after righteousness.

The cathedrals of England have developed a culture which goes some way to replacing what was lost in the life of the nation at the Dissolution of the Monasteries. In the so-called dark ages, Benedictine monasticism preserved what could be saved of the culture of Graeco-Roman antiquity and transmitted the gospel to the new nations of northern Europe and to succeeding generations. In our age, which is also characterised by new energies and new forms of barbarism, the cathedrals have a unique role in civilising and evangelising Europe with the music of God's word of life.

It is in this perspective that we should view the proposals currently before the Church for the reform of cathedrals, and it is precisely the relationship of cathedrals to culture in the broadest sense and a view of cathedrals as religious communities which I find under-emphasised in 'Heritage and Renewal – The Report of the Archbishops' Commission'.

Cathedrals have the possibility and therefore the duty to extend the scope of the mission of the people of God into aspects of human life which are rarely reached from a parochial base. In the long run it is the interpenetration of a whole culture by the gospel (the battle for the hearts and minds so disastrously lost by the Victorian Church at the height of its evangelical expansion) which furthers the kingdom. Cathedrals can fight some of the Church's battles on this front. They are closer to the main body of the people of God than are, for example, universities, and they are not potentially schismatic like some communities and house churches; but they must not be so absorbed in ecclesiastical concerns and structures or dominated by them that they lose their bridgeheads in the wider world or their opportunities for initiative and enterprise. One of the ways in which they do this, is by being religious communities, similar to, though not the same as, monastic houses.

How are all the good things upon which the Commission reports so appreciatively actually achieved? It is through the living of a common life, whereby it is those who work together, and pray together daily, eat and drink together frequently, who take decisions together, knowing that, in the execution of those decisions, they face the judgment of their peers, who are also their friends and neighbours.

Now I know that from the outside this looks very closed and clerical and oligarchical – but I do not think that it has been proved to be against the common good. I know too that this cannot be the case to the same extent in cathedrals of the old foundation or in parish church cathedrals where the canons, like the bishop, commute in from the suburbs. The implementation group will have to face at least the possibility that it will not be possible to devise a single form of governance to cover all forty-two cathedrals. But I can only give my personal testimony to my experience of cathedrals where the dean and chapter are the successors of a Benedictine prior and convent, in which a modified form of conventual life is more like conventional marriage than it is like conventional management.

The Report envisages cases where a cathedral may be in trouble and then the bishop and the diocese are there to help. That is good: but there is an alternative scenario whereby the bishop and the diocese face a crisis. Then a cathedral chapter with the confidence which can only come from habitually taking responsibility for its own decisions may have something to offer, precisely because it is not fully integrated into a hierarchical management structure but stands on its own feet.

We happen to be looking now at cathedrals; but we should not forget that it is the dioceses and the parishes which are stretched to breaking point in a system which may yet turn out to be unsustainable, as has happened in the whole areas of once Catholic France. Then an abbey, like the Abbey of Bec, can keep the faith and act as a minster for the surrounding countryside; but it can only do that if it can sustain its own life as a community with its own integrity and with the spirituality and common life which can alone give meaning to the motto: *Laborare est orare.* Work and prayer are inseparable notes in the music of God's word of life.

Notes

Editor's Introduction
1. Quoted in Michael de-la-Noy, *The Church of England, A Portrait*, London: Simon & Schuster, 1993, p. 159.

Chapter 1
1. Randle Manwaring, *From Controversy to Co-Existence: Evangelicals in the Church of England 1914–1980*, CUP, 1985, p. 55.
2. Kenneth Hylson-Smith, *Evangelicals in the Church of England 1734–1984*, T&T Clark, 1988, p. 334.
3. Not in October, as I inaccurately reported in my book *Evangelicals on the Move*, 1987.
4. *Churchman 91*, 1977, p. 102–13.
5. Timothy Bradshaw, *The Olive Branch*, Paternoster Press, 1990.

Chapter 2
1. *Christianity Today*, 12 September 1994, p. 23.
2. *The Nature of Christian Belief: A Statement and Exposition by the House of Bishops of the General Synod of the Church of England*, Church House Publishing, 1986.
3. *Church Statistics 1994: Some Facts and Figures about the Church of England*, The Central Board of Finance of the Church of England, 1994.
4. *Progressions*, January 1991, p. 21.
5. Ivan Illich quoted in Charles Handy, *Understanding Voluntary Organisations*, Penguin, 1990, p. 7.
6. S. J. Marriott, 'The Christian Order: The Soul of Man' in *Towards a Christian Order*, Eyre & Spottiswood, 1942, p. 28.

Chapter 3

1. John Moore argued at Swanwick in February 1994 that huge numbers would flock to REFORM if it dropped its opposition to women's leadership (*Church of England Newspaper*, March 1994, p. 15).

2. *The Nature of Christian Belief: A Statement and Exposition*, Church House Publishing, 1986. Michael Baughen has argued that this represents the only example in the 1980s of the House of Bishops acting collegially.

3. This is the argument of Robin Gill in *Beyond Decline*, SCM, 1988. Especially p. 72.

4. David Bebbington, *Evangelicalism in Modern Britain*, Routledge, 1993, p. 248.

5. Quoted in *Evangelicals Tomorrow* by John Capon, Fount, 1977.

6. ibid., chapter 3.

7. I am aware that the concept 'modernity' is a complex one. As David Harvey argues in *The Condition of Postmodernity* (Blackwell, 1990), modernity passed through various phases. I am therefore oversimplifying when I argue here that modernity equals the rationalism of Descartes and his twentieth-century disciple, A. J. Ayer.

8. James Barr was wrong to equate fundamentalism with evangelicalism, but he was surely correct to comment: 'The central feature of the classical fundamentalist doctrine seems to be that the Bible is part of a movement of true doctrine from God to man. It does not emerge from the community; rather it is directed towards the community and transmitted to the community by people like prophets and apostles.' *Fundamentalism*, SCM, 1981, p. 288.

9. Paul Avis, see note 17, chapter 2.

10. John Stott, *Contemporary Christian*, IVP, 1992, p. 211.

11. N. T. Wright, *The New Testament and the People of God*, SPCK, 1992, p. 450.

12. Dogma is of course vital in defining a core of belief. Tom Wright comments that 'Evangelical Anglicanism classically insists that the church has to be a teaching church and a

proclaiming church. She is therefore a "dogmatic" church: there is content to the faith that must be kept and proclaimed for each generation.' ibid., p. 152.

13. On Postmodernity, David Harvey's brilliant introduction, *The Condition of Postmodernity*, Blackwell, 1990, is highly recommended. For a stimulating account of the future of evangelicalism, see A. E. McGrath, *Evangelicalism and the Future of Christianity*, Hodder & Stoughton, 1994. The best analysis of evangelicalism remains David Babbington's *Evangelicalism in Modern Britain: A History from the 1730s to the 1980s*, London: Unwin Hyman, 1989.

14. Unfortunately there are no short and simple introductions to hermeneutics that I know of. Tony Thiselton's *New Horizons in Hermeneutics*, Marshall Pickering, 1992, is a mammoth and difficult book. Tony Thiselton has a brilliant grasp on a complex field. Sandra Schneider's *The Revelatory Text*, Harper Collins, 1991, is a shorter treatment of some of the key issues in biblical interpretation, but no less profound.

15. David Holloway quotes Hooker in a discussion document (REFORM, 1993), but manages to derive an opposite implication from Hooker's. Hooker intended this distinction to mean that we cannot judge who is in or out of the Church visible. REFORM want to make a clear-cut boundary on ethical, doctrinal and hence financial grounds. 'For lack of diligent observing the difference, first between the Church of God mystical and visible, then between the visible sound and corrupted, sometimes more, sometimes less, the oversights are neither few nor light that have been committed,' wrote Hooker. He also wrote: 'Now visible and invisible maketh, not two churches, but the divers estate and condition of the same church.' (*Of the Laws of Ecclesiastical Polity*, Book I p. 342, & V, lxviii, 6).

16. Sebastian Franck wrote: 'I am quite certain that for 1400 years now there has existed no gathered church and no sacrament.'

17. A. E. McGrath, *Reformation Thought: An Introduction*, Blackwell, 1993, p. 191.

18. For a detailed analysis of Reformation views of the Church see Paul D. L. Avis, *The Church in the Theology of the Reformers*, Basingstoke, 1981.

19. The Augsburg Confession of 1530, a Lutheran formulary, states: 'Est autem ecclesia congregatio sanctorum, in qua evangelicum recte docetur, et recte administratur sacramenta' (the Church is a congregation of the righteous in which the gospel is rightly taught and the sacraments rightly administered). Article XIX uses the word 'coetus' (literally 'coming together') rather than 'congregatio' for the English translation 'congregation'. This has led to a debate in the *Church Times* as to whether 'coetus' means 'the whole assembly of God' (the Bishop of Newcastle's view) or 'the local congregation' (David Holloway's view, a member of REFORM's Council) (*Church Times* of 19 and 25 November 1994). My original article of 12 November which provoked this exchange of letters took the view that 'the whole people of God' was left out of Article XIX but included in other Articles (such as Article XX or XXXIV), although I concede that my bishop has a point in arguing against David Holloway, for its implicit meaning in 'coetus'.

20. Oliver O'Donovan, *On the Thirty-nine Articles*, Paternoster, 1983, especially chapter 7.

21. W. H. Griffith Thomas, *The Principles of Theology*, Church Book Room Press, 1956, p. 288. Interestingly, he comments: 'An organised church is not the flock, but only one fold, so that no one community can be the church.' ibid., p. 276.

22. Bullinger, successor to Zwingli, put a hermeneutical slant to the preaching of the pure Word when he wrote: 'We embrace and retain the *true sense*.'

23. Paul Bradshaw comments in his excellent study of Evangelical Anglican Ecclesiology: 'The spiritual church is the physical, tangible and audible family of God. The church's spirituality cannot be regarded as the reverse of her physical historical being. When evangelicalism forgets this and identifies spiritual with invisible then it lapses into a form of pietism'. *The Olive Branch*, Paternoster, 1992, p. 141. We

must not confuse *spiritual* with *invisible*, nor must we confuse invisible and *universal*, as Michael Wilcock does in *The Church and the Churches*, St Nicholas' Church, 1994, p. 35.

24. Luther wasn't interested in 'the word that expels but the word that calls into the church'. He warned: 'you must not look for the church where there are no blemishes or flagrant faults'.

25. Here I follow the helpful typology of Stephen Sykes, *The Identity of Christianity*, London, SPCK, 1984, pp. 235–8. Sykes uses three models to clarify the identity of Christianity. The 'foundation-superstructure' model sees the foundation in early doctrinal and ministerial patterns, to which the Church refers back. This is similar to Cranmer's view during the English Reformation, and the Oxford Movement three hundred years later. The 'spirit-body' model sees the invisible spiritual life invigorating the visible organisation of the Church. The 'centre-circumference' model, mentioned here in the text, sees the Church as fulfilling its calling when it is closest to the Lord. This is close to Luther's position, although as I argue here, Luther was an Augustinian (the Church would continue to grow both wheat and tares), as was Calvin and most of the English Reformers. It is difficult to understand how REFORM can keep claiming the Reformation and English apologists such as Hooker as their authority.

26. Amongst the foremost academics in universities who describe themselves as evangelical, are Tony Thiselton, Dick France and Alister McGrath. Alister McGrath's output of popular books on subjects ranging from apologetics, the Reformation and the identity of evangelicalism has been prolific. Tony Thiselton has the most to give to this debate, but lack of time and the infinite ability to make things sound complicated prevent him doing so.

27. Lesslie Newbigin writes: 'A dialogue which is safe from all possible risks is no true dialogue. The Christian will go into dialogue believing that the sovereign power of the Spirit can use the occasion for the radical conversion of his partner *as*

well as himself.' Christian Witness in a Plural Society, BCC,
1977.
28. On this point, Michael Wilcock's pamphlet, *The Church
and the Churches*, St Nicholas' Church, 1994, seems very
close to the REFORM position. It reflects the tendency to
force texts to produce a meaning which contradicts the wider
context of the Bible, here by a word study on *ecclesia* (Greek
for church). In refusing to allow the Church to be both
visible and *catholic*, he falls into the very trap O'Donovan
(op. cit. above) warns us about.

Chapter 5

1. Richard Holloway, 'Thought on Preaching' in the College
of Preachers' Fellowship Paper No. 95, November 1993, p.
18–27.

Chapter 6

1. G. L. Carey, 'Lay ministry in a changing world' in *Sharing
a vision*, London: Darton, Longman and Todd, 1993, p. 200.
2. G. L. Carey, 'Leading the mission of the people of God'
in Gavin Reid (ed.), *Hope for the Church of England?*,
Eastbourne: Kingsway Publ., 1986, p. 172.
3. Chris McGillion, 'Another Anglican Crisis' in *The Tablet*,
5 November, 1994.
4. E. Schillebeeckx, *The Church with a Human Face*, New
York: Crossroad, 1985, p. 120.
5. R. Tiller and M. Birchall, *The Gospel Community and its
Leadership*, Basingstoke: Marshall Pickering, 1987, p. 49.
6. H. Benedict Green, *Lay Presidency at the Eucharist*, London:
Darton, Longman and Todd, 1994, p. 2.
7. World Council of Churches, *Baptism, Eucharist and Ministry*, p. 25.
8. Richard F. Holloway, 'Thoughts on Preaching', *College
of Preachers Fellowship Paper*, No. 95, November 1993, p.
19.
9. Schillebeeckx, op. cit. p. 119.

Chapter 7

1. P. Trible, *Texts of Terror: Literary Feminist Readings of Biblical Narratives*, Philadelphia: Fortress Press, 1978.
2. See the work of Janet Morley, *All Desires Known*, SPCK, 1988; and The St Hilda Community: *Women Included: A Book of Services and Prayers*, SPCK, 1991.
3. Fergus Kerr, 'Discipleship of Equals or Nuptial Mystery?' *New Blackfriars* 75:884, 1994, pp. 344–53.
4. Nicholas P. Harvey, 'Women's ordination: a sideways look', *Month*, 24:6, pp. 232–4.
5. Sandra Wilson, '"Which me will survive all these liberations?" . . . On Being a Black Woman Episcopal Priest', *Speaking of Faith: Global Perspectives on Women, Religion and Social Change*, ed. Diana L. Eck and Devaki Jain, Philadelphia: New Society Publishers, 1987, pp. 130–7.

Chapter 9

1. *Episcopal Ministry. The Report of the Archbishops' Group on the Episcopate*, Church House Publishing, 1990.
2. Op. cit., pp. 23, 24.
3. 'The Porvoo Common Statement', 1993; and 'The Porvoo Declaration', both publ. by The Council of Christian Unity of the General Synod of the Church of England, 1994.
4. In July, 1994.
5. Op. cit., p. 22.
6. Op. cit., p. 27.

Appendix A: The Keele Statement

Introduction to the Statement
by John R. W. Stott

The Congress Statement represents the common mind of the great majority of the almost 1,000 delegates who were present at Keele. It was composed by them, out of an original and entirely tentative draft, and knocked into shape paragraph by paragraph during many hours of discussion groups and plenary sessions. It is, therefore, a true child of the Congress as a whole.

In commending it to churchmen and churches for study, certain points need to be made clear:

1. The *Statement* must be not regarded as binding on the mind, conscience or action of any of the individuals present or the churches and societies they may have represented. It does not claim to be more than the consensus of the great majority.

2. The Congress delegates, by and large, were not experts but ordinary clergy and laity from the parishes. The *Statement* therefore expresses the convictions of a large but average evangelical constituency, rather than the fruits of a specialist study.

3. The Congress lasted only two and a half days. Although the period at our disposal was brief, we nevertheless thought it best to consider a wide range of subjects. We all wished we had more time to devote to every issue.

4. The mood of the Congress was one of penitence for past failures and of serious resolve for the future. This has meant for many of us not a change of fundamental position,

but of stance and even of direction. The *Statement* must not be taken, therefore, as our last and unalterable word. It is more a beginning than an end. As the situation develops, the dialogue increases and the issues clarify, we are sure that we will learn more, and we rather think that we have more to say. We certainly hope in future to be more flexible in our evangelical application of principle to policy.

Finally, we do not just commend the *Statement* for study, but for study *with a view to action*. The worst fate which can befall any conference is to watch its findings dissipate in mere talk. But the *Statement* calls for action, in some places for precise action. We earnestly hope that individual clergy and laity, parish study groups and Parochial Church Councils will consider how the *Statement* could and should be implemented in their own local situation.

The Congress Statement

1. The Church and its Message

1. We affirm our belief in the historic faith of the Church, in an age in which it has come under attack from both outside and inside the Church. We value the creeds and the thirty-nine articles as expressions of that faith. In acknowledgement of the Lordship of Jesus Christ we make this confession of faith.

THE GOD WE WORSHIP

The Living God

2. We affirm that God, as proclaimed in the Christian gospel, is the sovereign creator and sustainer of the universe. Not only does He control all ordinary events by His providence, but He also displays His power to restore and recreate in supernatural events of saving significance: particularly in the incarnation, resurrection and miracles of Jesus, the inspiration of Holy Scripture, and the new creation. God reveals Himself as triune – Father, Son and Holy Spirit. As such, He is both Lord and restorer of His world.

God in Jesus Christ

3. The Christian message proclaims God in Jesus Christ, incarnate, crucified, raised, ascended, reigning, and coming again. He is God's final word to man and therefore the message concerning Him is in this respect unchangeable. We affirm that Christianity is more than a system of beliefs and a way of behaviour; essentially it is a person-to-person relationship with God in Jesus Christ. We reject attempts to drive a wedge between 'the Jesus of history' and 'the Christ of faith'.

The Christ of the Scriptures
4. The Christ whom we worship and proclaim is the Christ of
all the Scriptures. We acknowledge God's redemptive words
and deeds, recorded in the Old Testament and in the apostolic
witness of the New Testament as essential to the full testimony
to Christ. And we interpret and confess Christ in terms of the
total teaching of both Testaments.

THE AUTHORITY OF THE BIBLE

Revelation
5. Revelation is by word as well as by deed. God reveals
Himself not only in mighty acts but also in the word by
which He interprets those acts. We therefore receive the Bible
as authoritative divine teaching, and conclude that to differ
from the Bible is to deviate from the truth.

Inspiration
6. Scripture expresses one great theme under a rich variety of
style, background and forms. It is one because it expresses one
mind, that of God the Holy Spirit who inspired it. The authority of Scripture derives not merely from its subject-matter,
but also from the fact that it is itself the Word of God,
written by virtue of a unique operation of the Holy Spirit,
enlightening, prompting and controlling its human authors.
Scripture is the supreme authority in all matters of faith
and practice both for the Church and for the individual.
It is also the means of grace through which God reveals
Himself in present experience.

We affirm that the supreme agent of biblical interpretation is God the Holy Spirit, who directs Christians in their
search to understand the message of God. This message was
given through the minds of the biblical writers, and must be
considered in relation to their personal, social, and national
situations. We welcome all scholarship which promotes a more
precise understanding of holy Scripture. Thus we confess our
faith that the Scriptures are the wholly trustworthy oracles of
God.

MAN, SIN AND GRACE

Man under sin

7. God made man to know, love and serve Him and his fellow men, but man rejects all these purposes and is thus in a state of rebellion and alienation. This affront to the Holy God is reflected in the human situation where man, and not God, is made supreme. And it is displayed in the social disarray of the human race, the psychological maladjustment of individuals, and the whole range of human sin and crime. We therefore reject all optimism about human nature without Christ, holding that without His grace all men, under the influence of sin and a personal evil being, make evil choices.

Redemption

8. We affirm that the message of Christ is a proclamation of God's love, justice and power, assured to us in the cross and resurrection. In Jesus Christ, God the creator has taken action to redeem and rescue man from sin and evil, and to restore him to fellowship with Himself. Thus the Gospel is a message of undeserved grace to hopeless and helpless sinners.

A full Christian redemption results in the active renewal both of the individual, physically, mentally and spiritually, and also of society, in terms of love and justice. Furthermore, it involves the use of the material world for God's glory and man's benefit. Nothing less than this does justice to the New Testament idea of the supremacy of Christ in His world, and to His full saving redemption.

Atonement

9. The law of God reveals Him as a righteous judge who justly condemns sin. The atonement can be fully understood only when Christ is seen as bearing the penalty of our sins in our place. This is the deepest, though not the only, significance of the divine love demonstrated in the cross. Upon this depends man's conquest of Satan and the powers of evil. Interpretations which omit this element reflect an inadequate view of God's holy character and also of the greatness of the grace

and love whereby God Himself met the claims of His own
justice.

Justification
10. We affirm that both Christ's sacrifice for sin and also our
justification from sin, which is grounded on it, are finished
works. Justification is God's acceptance of believers as righteous in Christ and His adoption of them into a covenant family
relationship with Himself. It is received by faith as a gift and is
final and irrevocable. God constantly renews His invitations
and promises to Christians even when they fail Him.

Response
11. Whereas God in the gospel commands all men to repent
and believe, and offers salvation freely to all who do, not all
men accept His grace. Scripture has no place for a universal
salvation, or for the possibility of a further successful probation in a future life for those who reject Christ in this. A
persistent and deliberate rejection of Jesus Christ condemns
men to hell.

THE NEW LIFE
Conversion
12. In the supernatural creative act of God in the historical
resurrection of Jesus there emerged a new spiritual order. It
both effected the union of the Church with the risen Christ
and pledges the final resurrection of the believer. It also
leads to the manifestation of the newness of life which begins in the Christian's new birth. Evidence of his new life
is seen in repentance and faith in Christ, and in the growing fruit of the Spirit. Conversions are not always of the
same pattern, but regeneration cannot be presumed where
such signs of new life are lacking.

Baptism and Holy Communion, the sacraments of the
gospel, pledge to us the blessings which are ours in Christ
through His death and resurrection. Baptism affirms God's
justifying work in Christ and Holy Communion the riches of

His resources for our growth in grace. Both point forward to the Christian's final salvation.

Christian behaviour

13. The Holy Spirit is given to us in regeneration, enabling us to love God's law and empowering us to keep it. Thus we affirm that for a Christian to keep God's law is not an external legalism but the expression of his true nature, and also of his love and gratitude for salvation. At the same time, we confess that legalistic attitudes have in the past obscured our witness to Christian liberty and we see 'situation ethics'* as warning us against doctrinaire and insensitive attitudes to people's needs. Nevertheless there is a form of 'situation ethics' which is in effect altogether lawless since it disregards God's moral law in scripture and fails to realise the inability of love as a motive to set standards for itself and achieve them.

The longing for human dignity and decency which lies behind many present-day forms of cultural revolt, needs the gospel message of sin and grace, with its summons to self-denial and bond-service to Jesus Christ. This is the only foundation for true humanism, and the only avenue to authentic freedom.

Spiritual Gifts

14. We thank God for creating in us a hunger to seek the best gifts of the Spirit in fullest possible measure, and we rejoice at every sign of His working in human lives. In this connection, however, we have no united opinion as to whether current 'charismatic'* manifestations are of the same sort as the corresponding New Testament 'gifts of the Spirit' or not.

THE HOLY SPIRIT IN THE CHURCH
The World-wide Church

15. The Church is a divinely created community, and a fellowship of those who through the Holy Spirit have received the benefits of the gospel. As God's people, redeemed by Jesus Christ, the Church is called forth to share in the mission of

the Spirit to the whole world. It is essential to the life of the Church to set forth the word of God in accordance with the Bible, to dispense the sacraments of Baptism and the Lord's Supper, and to administer discipline in the interest of the Church's character of holiness and love. All ministry is the gift of Christ in His Church. Whatever its structure, it should always provide oversight, eldership and service.

The Local Church
16. The local church, the community of Christian people in each place, must manifest the Lordship of the Holy Spirit in fellowship, prayer and mutual service; in holiness of life; in reverence for the scriptures and the sacraments as means through which Christ, when sought, may be found; in openness to welcome others, with readiness to share both spiritual and material things to meet their needs; and in flexibility of structure, so that pastoral and evangelistic effectiveness is not impeded by out-of-date procedures. We confess our own great failures here, and call on the whole Anglican Church to pray for a fresh outpouring of the Holy Spirit to re-vitalise its congregational life.

THE CHRISTIAN HOPE
17. Acknowledging God as the Lord of events, and history as the unfolding of His plan, we look for the promised personal return of Jesus Christ and we call on all Christian people to live in expectation of it and readiness for it. We look forward to the resurrection of the body, and to the final consummation of all things in Christ and their restoration to the Father, that God may be all in all.

2. The Church and its Mission

The source of mission
18. Mission originates in the nature of God. It is the activity by which He works to restore the world to harmony with Himself.

It is the work of God the Father, who is always active in saving love and in judgment within His rebellious world. It is the work of God the Son, in whom God has reconciled the world to Himself, and through whom alone men are redeemed. It is the work of God the Spirit, who testifies to the world of God's redeeming love, and by His recreative action brings sinful men to know Christ personally and to find in Him new life.

Our part in mission
19. God graciously calls the Church to share in His mission, and all Christians are involved in this calling. Mission is therefore not a technique by which the Church expands itself, nor is it a venture belonging to the Church. Every Christian has experienced the saving love of Christ and has received the gift of the Spirit. His zeal for God's glory, his gratitude to Christ, his compassion for people, and his obedience to the Lord, all impel him to take his part in the mission of God, which extends to all people in all places until the return of Christ.

The scope of mission
20. God's purpose is to make men new through the gospel, and through their transformed lives to bring all aspects of human life under the Lordship of Christ. Christians share in God's work of mission by being present among non-Christians to live and to speak for Christ, and in His name to promote justice and meet human need in all its forms. Evangelism and compassionate service belong together in the mission of God.

THE TASK TODAY
The local church
21. The work of mission is the work of the whole people of God, not only of missionary specialists. The responsibility for mission to the whole community rests primarily on the local church. The missionary task will only be accomplished as Christians learn to fulfil their calling to bear witness at work and at home. For this, specific training is required.

We welcome the great evangelistic campaigns of our day.

We recognise them as complementary to continuous personal and congregational evangelism.

World mission
22. The missionary task confronting local churches is the same the world over. It is as urgent in Britain as it is everywhere else. Yet in many parts of the world the Church is a small segment of the population, and weak in many ways. It therefore needs to share the greater resources of manpower and money which are ours, and we should not grudge to give of them. At the same time, the Church in Britain is in great need of the spiritual vigour which God has given in many parts of the Church overseas; we long that this might be imparted to us also.

Missionaries
23. While every Christian is called to witness, this is not to say that every Christian is called to be a missionary. A missionary, strictly speaking, is called by God and sent by the Church to be part of its outreach in a country, a society, or a culture other than his own. The missionary vocation is distinctive, and a missionary requires a supporting organisation and fellowship, in partnership with his home church.

It is the responsibility of the local churches to keep this vocation before people.

'Secular missionaries'
24. We call for an increased willingness on the part of Christians in Britain to enter employment overseas in government service or in commerce, when by so doing they can strengthen the Church in other lands, or witness where missionaries are excluded. By extending their fellowship to such people missionary societies can greatly encourage them in their spiritual lives. The fellowship of Christians from overseas who are working in this country is an enrichment to the life of the Church. Such persons must be sought out, welcomed, and given Christian care and love.

Missionary Societies

25. We affirm that missionary societies, as autonomous voluntary agencies, are, in the present situation, the best means by which the Church of England may engage in mission to the whole world. We urge missionary societies of like evangelical conviction, including the home mission societies, to seek ways of working in closer co-operation. In particular, we recommend to the Congress Committee that a suitable working party be set up to explore definite starting points. We believe that closer co-operation will help in world-wide missionary strategy.

Priorities in world mission

26. We recognise that missionary societies are called to work in partnership with the national Churches, where these exist, and that in some nations today this partnership demands patient and disciplined self-limitation on the missionaries' part. The training of national leaders is therefore a fundamental priority, and national Churches are asking for our full co-operation in this.

The Church also has to face the challenges of accelerating urbanisation, the exploding student population and the opportunity for evangelism among overseas students in this country. In addition, we see a continuing need for pioneer evangelism in many parts of the world.

Evangelism in Britain

27. The missionary situation in many parts of Britain, particularly in industrial inner city and new housing areas, calls for special action. We have to admit to our shame that the Church has so far largely failed these areas.

We urge that dioceses will designate special mission areas, calling for support from the wider Church, and the maximum flexibility in matters of organisation and liturgy.

We affirm our faith that God is able to create and maintain local leadership in any community. Until such local leaders emerge, mission areas can best be served by specialised teams, including full and part-time, clerical and lay members. We welcome the willingness of some Christians to move out of their natural social environment into such areas.

We strongly recommend that some clergy and laity should be recognised and supported by the Church as full-time evangelists.

Mission and other faiths

28. We affirm the unique claims of Jesus Christ to be the only Saviour, through whom alone men can be saved, and deprecate the current tendency to equate all religions as ways which eventually lead to God. We welcome sympathetic dialogue with their adherents, but we reject as misleading the statement that Christ is already present in other faiths. We cannot regard those true insights which non-Christian religions contain as constituting a way of salvation. It is scriptural to speak in this connection of the work of the Holy Spirit preparing men of other faiths for the gospel.

COMMUNICATION

Person-to-person

29. A very effective and scriptural form of evangelism takes place when a Christian, in genuine friendship with his non-Christian neighbour, interprets the good news of salvation to him. The supreme importance of person-to-person relationships must be stressed in all communication of the gospel. One of the most natural meeting places for such communication is the home. Christians should practice hospitality.

Teaching and proclamation

30. In many areas, even in Britain, we cannot assume any accurate knowledge of Christian teaching. We accept our responsibility to provide basic instruction for all age groups, including adults. Alongside other methods of communication, we continue to regard preaching as indispensable.

Language and content
31. We accept the challenge and must submit to the discipline of making the gospel intelligible and relevant in our day, without distorting its biblical content.

Literature
32. We recognise the urgent need particularly in the younger nations for Christian reading matter including especially the translation and distribution of the Bible. We call for generous support for Christian literature projects overseas, including the training of national writers. We also call for renewed efforts to produce and distribute literature for those in our land who are not used to reading solid blocks of print.

Radio and television
33. We welcome the increasing use of radio and television in presenting the gospel throughout the world. We urge Christians to pray and pay for more religious broadcasting time, and we invite the national broadcasting concerns to seek more effective means of meeting the spiritual need in our nation. We encourage Christians to develop their skills as script writers and broadcasters. We also call for imaginative planning for the use of local radio.

CONCERN FOR MISSION

Renewal for mission
34. A church spiritually renewed is a church renewed for mission. A cord of missionary zeal has three strands: love for the Lord who died for the world, obedience to His command, and informed concern for the world for which He died. A church begins seriously to share in world mission only when it becomes concerned to evangelise continuously within its own neighbourhood and community. So we call on Christians everywhere to pray for deep spiritual renewal in the Church as a whole, and we seek renewal for ourselves as Evangelicals within the Church of England.

Informed concern
35. Spiritual renewal needs to be accompanied by increased knowledge about the world and about mission. Misunderstanding of the biblical summons to 'separation from the world' has sometimes diverted Evangelicals from grasping, or even giving thought to, the nature of the world and the contemporary situation. We call on all Evangelicals to study and be involved in the contemporary world, so that prayer and action can be intelligently related to it. We urge Evangelicals both in theological colleges and in parishes to study and to teach the missionary implications of Christian doctrine.

Costly involvement
36. In view of the extreme urgency of the situation both at home and overseas, we call upon all Christians to give themselves earnestly to prayer. Among the priorities are prayer for those parts of the Church which are closed to outside help, or are suffering persecution; prayer for a recovery of courage and initiative in evangelism by the local churches in every land; and prayer for the Lord to provide more workers and supporters for His mission.

All this demands a level of sacrificial giving which we have not yet reached. The Old Testament tithe should be regarded as a minimum standard for Christian giving, and a due proportion of this should be set aside for mission. This should apply to individuals and to local churches. Finally, we enjoin upon ourselves and our churches total commitment to the task of proclaiming Christ throughout the world in our generation.

3. The Church and the World

37. We believe that our evangelical doctrines have important ethical implications. But we confess to our shame that we have not thought sufficiently deeply or radically about the problems of our society. We are therefore resolved to give ourselves to more study of these crucial issues in future.

CHRISTIAN INVOLVEMENT

38. This is God's world in spite of its invasion by evil. He cares for it and so must we. The Church is set in the world by God Himself, who has made us both citizens of our country and ambassadors for Christ. We must therefore work not only for the redemption of individuals, but also for the reformation of society.

THE CHURCH AND THE NATION

Christians in society

39. We recognise that the civil authority has a divinely ordained rôle in the ordering of society to maintain law and justice, to defend its citizens, and to create conditions conducive to the material and moral well-being of all. As a member of society the Christian is called both to support the State in all rightful activity and to challenge it in the areas where its responsibilities are not being fulfilled. The dignity of man through creation and redemption, and the duty to love one's neighbour, make every political, social and moral problem a matter of concern to the Church.

This concern may be expressed in four ways: by individual Christian action in daily life; by playing a full part with others in secular activities; by voluntary Christian societies; and by the work of the Church corporately.

We therefore give particular encouragement to Christians to regard participation in local and national politics as a Christian vocation. We also hold that it is often a Christian duty to speak out when occasion requires Christian comment. We encourage Christians to write to, and for, the local and national press on such occasions.

'A caring community'

40. Christians should be involved with people at every social level. The Church should be a caring community, welcoming in Christ's name addicts, criminals, the hungry, the homeless and all in need. More important than any specific proposal is our concern to recover a vision of the Church involved

prayerfully and sacrificially in all the problems raised by an affluent, leisured but bewildered society.

MORALITY AND LEGISLATION
Legislation
41. The Church must be loyal to God's absolute standards and practical in its application of them to legislation. We maintain that the law of our land still primarily reflects Christian morality, but we recognise that the full Christian ethic cannot be enforced by law.

Divorce and abortion
42. The law of divorce provides a case in point. Christ unequivocally stated that God's purpose for man was lifelong fidelity in marriage, but He in no way suggested that the Mosaic concession to the 'hardness of men's hearts' was not made by divine permission. This does not mean that we believe in two standards, one for Christians and the other for non-Christians. We accept one fundamental standard, but we believe that we may rightly take our part in framing a civil law of divorce which will best combine such concessions to human frailty and sin as the circumstances of society may require, with maintenance of the greatest possible stability in marriage.

Similarly, in regard to abortion, we judge that the life of the mother and her physical and mental health, must have priority over the potential personality of the foetus. We therefore urge that questions such as alleged rape, the possibility that the embryo might be malformed, and social considerations, should not be regarded as grounds for abortion unless the mother's health is in danger.

The problem of abortion troubles so many minds and consciences that it merits investigation by a Royal Commission.

VOLUNTARY ACTION IN THE WELFARE STATE
43. We welcome the existence of the Welfare State. We regard it as an acceptance by the State of its responsibility under God. We also welcome the increase in various forms

of voluntary action. There are, however, still inadequacies and gaps in welfare services. We urge national and local governments to take the necessary steps in such matters. In the meantime, Christians have a duty to show their love and concern in a variety of ways. There will, indeed, always be a need for the love and compassion which are personal rather than institutional in character. The visiting and aftercare of prisoners, mental rehabilitation, and care for the lonely and aged, are a few among many areas in which the compassionate ministry of the Church should go hand in hand with efforts to make the State take effective action. The evidence is that members of local churches do not take this responsibility seriously.

LAND AND HOUSING

44. The hardship caused by the high price of land and property, the shortage of houses and of low rental accommodation, and other factors give us much concern. We fully endorse the aims of the recently formed Christian organisation SHELTER but we recognise that only the State can deal with the overall problem, in the solution of which Christians ought to play their full part.

EDUCATION

45. We affirm that Christians have a vital rôle to play in education, and we wish to contribute to all discussions on the structure of the schools of our country (for example in the fields of comprehensive education, and the continuance of alternative fee-paying schools).

Religious education in schools can be justified on education grounds, and we note that it has strong support in opinion polls. But we recognise the right of every parent to withdraw his child from this instruction on conscientious grounds, as well as to choose the school in which his child will be educated.

Christian education in Church and State schools is in danger of going by default for lack of an adequate supply of convinced and qualified Christian teachers, both in the schools and colleges of education. We therefore call upon Christians to place the vocation of Christian teaching before young people.

The modern tendency to set in opposition a content-centred* and a child-centred* education poses a false antithesis. What is needed is child-related, Christ-centred education.

HUMAN PROBLEMS IN A TECHNICAL AGE

46. We welcome the advance of technology as an aspect of man's dominion over the created order, while recognising that in both industrial and rural communities it brings great changes in the pattern of human life. Both Church and State ought to be alert to the peculiar human problems which arise, particularly in towns largely dependent on one particular industry, from the movement and closure of industries which often results from technological development. An expansion in retraining facilities is urgently needed. Management faces severe temptations to be callous and to treat men as dispensable pieces of machinery, and Trade Unions face increasing temptation to hold industry to ransom. In such situations the Church must uphold the principle of social justice and the dignity of man.

WORK AND LEISURE

47. Work is God's plan for man since the creation, and is a means by which we share in His creative activity. We are called to glorify God in our work and to minister to the needs of society. Such an attitude to work is a gateway to personal fulfilment, and is also the long-term cure for the serious economic problems of our country, where the frequent absence of a sense of duty in relation to work is a cause of grave concern.

A responsible attitude to work must be balanced by a responsible attitude to leisure. The great danger of excessive overtime and weekend working is that the health of the worker and the well-being of his family will be seriously impaired. We must remind the State of the great wisdom of the creation ordinance of one day's rest in seven. Sunday should be safe-guarded as the national day of rest.

War

48. War is essential evil, being a manifestation of man's fallen nature. It is the urgent duty of Christians to pursue all means to maintain, or where necessary to restore, peace with justice and freedom.

We nevertheless recognise that it is a government's first duty to uphold law and justice and that even war may be justified as resistance to aggression or restraint of such manifest evils as genocide.

The agonising question for the Christian today is whether there could ever be an evil worse than indiscriminate nuclear warfare. We urge that nuclear weapons should be effectively banned by all countries, but would hesitate to advocate uni-lateral disarmament.

Race Relations

49. We affirm that all mankind is one in the sight of God. We therefore condemn racial discrimination in all countries and are especially concerned at the appearance of it in our own country in the spheres of employment and accommodation. We support all constructive policies and efforts to improve relations between groups and individuals of different races.

The Church must demonstrate that its members are all one in Christ Jesus and reiterate in this context our Lord's command to love our neighbour. The Good Samaritan did not choose his neighbour. Christians who are themselves preju-diced must look to Christ to set them free. They should support community relations councils where these exist and they should recognise a citizen's right to express his own culture.

The Developing Nations

50. Many parts of the world are already overpopulated; and

hunger, poverty and starvation are widespread. Food production is inadequate and its distribution inequitable. Through government action, the better developed nations should be prepared to make far greater sacrifices for the less fortunate countries. We support the Pope's suggestion of a world fund and we recommend study of the British Council of Churches' report on world poverty. We urge our government to make a more generous contribution to developing countries and we pledge our support.

We are concerned that in some nations ignorance, superstitions, or even religious beliefs are obstacles both to the fullest use of food resources, and to the control of population. We believe that God has entrusted to man the responsibility for controlling procreation, and we hold that contraception is morally right when responsibly used. We believe that the whole Church should encourage an enlightened attitude to these issues.

OTHER PROBLEMS
Sexual Morality
51. Whilst sympathising with young people concerning certain social customs and the resulting temptations which press upon them today, we assert that marriage is the divinely ordained state in which complete sexual fulfilment is to be sought. Premarital and extra-marital intercourse are therefore contrary to this principle and are responsible for much unhappiness.

We urge local churches to provide adequate instruction about sex and sexual morality, both for young people in general and for engaged couples in particular, and we believe that self-control should be encouraged as the basis of future family happiness and stability.

Addiction
52. We are deeply concerned about all forms of addiction in this country today and in particular that of drug addiction. We urge that the following preventive measures be taken: *i*. helping parents and teachers to recognise the beginnings

of addiction, through parent-teacher association courses; *ii.* teaching young people the dangers of addiction; *iii.* supporting the government in the measures it takes to prevent it. The position is so grave that we also call for funds to provide more centres, and we encourage pilot schemes for rehabilitation of addicts. And we refer this to the Congress Committee. We recognise that rehabilitation requires expert medical and psychiatric treatment, compassionate involvement by Christians, and a true experience of Christian conversion which alone can transform and really satisfy.

4. The Church and its Structures

53. The Church is one people. The difference between clergy and laity is one of function. Ordination is a calling and gift of Christ by His Spirit in His Church, which sets a man apart to the ministry of the Word and Sacraments and of pastoral care. He is therein given authority and power so to minister, but his status is not otherwise altered. Ministry is to be exercised by the whole people of God, and this must be seen in the life of the Church at both local and national level.

THE CHURCH AT THE LOCAL LEVEL
The Parochial System
54. A parochial system which provides comprehensive geographical coverage of the country, gives the kind of framework within which the local church may best fulfil its responsibilities of worship and witness. Particularly is this so in respect of its evangelistic responsibility. But we fully recognise that in some urban areas the present parish boundaries have ceased to correspond to natural groupings. Therefore we need to be ready to accept the rearranging of boundaries where this is plainly necessary.

Grouping of Parishes
55. We call for more co-operation between parishes. We have

no desire to perpetuate a spirit of isolationism, although we submit that group* and team* ministries create special difficulties when there are deep theological differences. We commend the idea of voluntary groupings to parishes, even where such theological differences exist, with a view to greater fellowship and the pooling of resources. We recognise that we could well benefit in this way from others of a different theological persuasion. But we ask that those drawing up schemes for group and team ministries under the Pastoral Measure should take full account of conscientious doctrinal convictions held by the clergy and laity of the parishes involved.

Patterns of Ministry

56. We are convinced that we should aim in every area to create indigenous congregations with authorised ministers and full lay participation in evangelistic, pastoral, and administrative matters. We need to encourage much more flexible and specialised patterns of ministry, both of men and women. We should think not only in terms of 'order' but also in terms of recognising spiritual gifts.

We therefore welcome such experiments as 'Part-time' ministries, lay eldership schemes and House Churches with lay leadership. We urge that steps be taken to enlarge still further the area of lay participation, provided that the continuing need of men for the ordained ministry is not overlooked. The size of a church's staff (which ought to include secretarial help) should be determined, not by its wealth, but by its needs.

Alongside the Parochial System we call for additional special structures to serve particular sections of the community, e.g. the homeless, alcoholics and drug addicts.

THE CHURCH AT THE NATIONAL LEVEL

Bishops

57. We welcome the suggestion of reorganising Dioceses in order to free the bishop from excessive administrative burdens, so that he may exercise more effective pastoral oversight.

Synodical Government*
58. We welcome the prospect of clergy and laity serving together on an equal basis in Synods. We appreciate the work of the Hodson Commission and their report *Government by Synod*. While accepting their proposals in general as the way forward, we would recommend the following:
(a) In the General Synod the number of laity should in principle equal the number of clergy, including bishops.
(b) The ex-officio element in the General Synod should be kept to a minimum.
(c) Each parish should be represented directly on the Diocesan Synod.
(d) The bishop's right to withdraw any matter appearing to him to belong essentially to his episcopal office or pastoral duties must be more clearly defined and then re-examined. A substantial minority of congress delegates wanted this proposed right altogether deleted.
(e) All electoral rolls should be entirely reconstituted in 1969 and every five years thereafter by renewed application.

Establishment*
59. We recognise afresh that the National Church which we have inherited presents us with pastoral advantages and as such gives us opportunities to serve the nation. We judge that modifications in the establishment should be delayed until Synodical Government has given the laity a full and effective share in the government of the Church.

The Image of the Church
60. Our primary concern must be with what God thinks of the Church, not with what men think. Nevertheless, we are concerned that many obstacles to evangelism are created by such things as the archaism of our language, the dress of our clergy, the quality of our publicity and the state of our premises.

Appointment to Parishes
61. We call for action on the following issues:
(a)   The part played by local churches in appointments,
         including Crown appointments, should be extended.
         We recommend that, when a vacancy occurs, the church
         be visited by the Patron or his representative for the
         purpose of full consultation.
(b)   It should be possible for men who wish to move from
         their present post, to have their names placed on a
         confidential list available to all Patrons.

Patronage*
62. Most Patrons show understanding of, and devotion to, the
needs of the livings for which they are responsible. We believe
that Patronage Trusts and Societies are a proper means of
ensuring that the interests of the vacant parish take priority. Furthermore, they are an important safeguard against
the possibility of bureaucratic and unfeeling management of
appointments. In spite of the administrative neatness of Regional Boards, as proposed in the Paul Report, we question
whether they could give adequate consideration to the needs
of individual parishes.

Conclusion
63. Whilst we have put forward positive suggestions for making the structures of the Church more relevant to the needs of
the present age, we recognise that such action cannot in itself
bring the renewal of the Church for which we long. For this we
depend wholly on the working of the Holy Spirit of God.

5. The Church and its Worship

Ministry and worship
64. Worship Godward and witness manward together constitute the duty of the whole Church. The ministry of Word and
Sacrament in the power of the Holy Spirit enables the body

of Christ to understand and receive God's salvation in all its fullness, to respond to God in praise and self-surrender, and to be renewed corporately for its task of mission in the world.

Our failures
65. We acknowledge that in the past we have not achieved these ideals. We have failed to maintain the Unity of Word and Sacrament. While rightly exalting preaching, we have underrated the evangelical function of the sacrament of the Lord's Supper as a visible word. We have been suspicious of experimentation and frightened of change, and have tended to individualism. Furthermore, we have been slow to learn from other parts of God's Church.

LITURGICAL REVISION
Attitudes to revision
66. Liturgical revision is long overdue. Much as we value the doctrinal basis of the services of 1662, we are not so wedded to their structures, contents or language as not to see the need for new forms. Some of us desire these new forms to be a conservative revision of the present services; some desire services in modern language, and strongly urge the provision of such forms for an experimental period; while others are looking for something much more radical, though retaining the same doctrinal position as 1662. But to all the period of experiment is welcome. No alarms should accompany the loosening of a legal uniformity, although we believe that the ideal of Common Prayer should not be forgotten.

New Testament theology makes the local church corporately responsible for ordering and offering worship aright. The Prayer Book (Alternative and Other Services) Measure gives responsibility to Parochial Church Councils to consent or otherwise to the use of new forms of service in any church in a parish. We therefore call on incumbents and Parochial Church Councils to study the proposed services, in order to discharge their biblical and legal responsibility in this matter. The resultant local variations in worship should not cause

Christians to take offence when they move from one part
of the country to another. Equally, local churches should
not give offence by unlawful innovations. We call on all
local churches to abide by the present law, even where it
seems irksome. We ourselves will seek reform only by lawful
means.

Biblical basis
67. The proper basis of liturgical revision is not the practice of the second and third centuries, but the teaching of
the Bible applied with reference to contemporary needs and
in the light of existing services.

Liturgical commission services
68. We consider that the services presented by the Liturgical
Commission have many excellent features structurally, and,
in the case of the new Baptism and Confirmation Services,
linguistically. However, certain doctrinal points in some of
the proposed services cause serious objections. For example:
the Initiation Services overvalue Confirmation; the Burial
Service fails to express Christian assurance and hope; the Holy
Communion service in its present form includes an offering of
the bread and the cup to God and explicit petitions for the
departed, and contains no adequate reference to the Second
Coming.

In the case of Holy Communion, we desire that the service
should more clearly affirm its grounding in the once-for-all
sacrifice of Christ upon the Cross; it can be spoken of in
sacrificial terms only in the sense that it embraces the re-
sponsive self-offering of believers in gratitude for Christ's
finished work of sin-bearing. We share the longing, voiced
on several occasions in the Church Assembly, for liturgy that
will be consistently biblical and consequently unifying. We
affirm our readiness to enter into dialogue with those from
whom we differ, with a view to finding the best way of securing
such liturgy.

THE MINISTRY OF THE WORD

Priority of preaching

69. We call on the Church to set the highest standards for the ministry of the Word, to proclaim the whole counsel of God, and to recover an eager expectation of receiving grace through this means. Preaching is the authoritative proclamation of the Word of God, applied by the Spirit, demanding decision rather than discussion. We therefore regard the development of techniques of discussion and dialogue for Christian instruction as a useful adjunct to preaching, but not as a substitute for it.

Preaching standards

70. The whole Church must co-operate if the proper functioning of preaching is to be recovered in our day. Colleges must give deeper and balanced training in theology, communication and psychology. Ministers must discover the needs of their congregations with a view to relevant preaching. Congregations must set their ministers free to devote themselves to prayer and ministry of the Word. Preachers must avail themselves of every opportunity to improve their preaching.

THE MINISTRY OF THE SACRAMENTS – I. HOLY BAPTISM

Baptism is the sign and seal of covenant-relationship between God and His people.

Infant baptism

71. We affirm our belief in the scriptural foundation of infant baptism, but declare that only the children of parents who profess to be Christians are fit subjects for this rite. Indiscriminate infant baptism, as commonly practised in England, is a scandal, and is incidentally productive of much of the current divisive reaction against the baptising of infants. We call now for a theologically-inspired national practice of baptismal discipline.

We must be welcoming to little children, as Jesus was. But we deny the propriety of baptising the infants of parents who do not profess to be Christians themselves and who cannot promise to bring up their children as Christians. We approve the proposals regarding Christian parenthood and upbringing which are embodied in the Preface to the new Service for Infant Baptism.

In view of the widespread misunderstanding caused by such expressions as 'this child is regenerate', we would welcome their revision, provided that the covenant basis which they express is not lost.

Public baptism
72. We urge that baptism should always be held at public services of the Church, unless there are compelling reasons to the contrary. The baptismal liturgies of the Church of England need further revision to enable whole families to be baptised together with one rite.

Confirmation
73. Christian initiation is sacramentally complete in baptism. The confirmation of those baptised as adults should be combined with their baptism, as proposed by the Liturgical Commission. But the declarations of repentance and faith which are made in infant baptism need to be ratified by the child at the age of discretion. This ratification may be accompanied appropriately by the laying on of hands, although this act is not essential to the service.

Admission to Communion
74. We call for further theological study as to whether the age of discretion is always the right time for admission to Holy Communion. Some of us would like the children of Christian families to be admitted as communicants at an early age, provided that there is adequate baptismal discipline.

Rebaptism*
75. We reject rebaptism as unscriptural. It is destructive of the sacrament, makes it a sign of our faith rather than of God's

grace, and removes its once-for-all character. It is also hurtful
to the unity of God's people.

THE MINISTRY OF THE SACRAMENTS – II. HOLY COMMUNION
Its centrality
76. We have failed to do justice in our practice to the twin
truths that the Lord's Supper is the main service of the people
of God, and that the local church, as such, is the unit within
which it is properly administered. This is not to undervalue
in any way attendance at other services of the day, but to
admit that we have let the sacrament be pushed to the outer
fringes of church life, and the ministry of the Word be divorced
from it. Small communion services have been held seemingly
at random, often more than one a Sunday, and the whole
local church seldom or never comes together at the Lord's
Table. As individuals we have lacked both a concern that
the local church should amend its ways, and also a personal discipline of attendance.

We determine to work towards the practice of a weekly
celebration of the sacrament as the central corporate service
of the church, and some of us would recommend the use of
'one loaf' (1 Corinthians 10.17) as biblical and symbolic of
that corporate unity.

Participation
77. Authorised lay people, in addition to Readers, should
assist by reading the lessons, by leading the intercessions, by
preaching and by administering both elements.

The Position of the minister
78. We believe that the minister should stand where he may
break bread before the people. We commend consideration of
the westward position.

THE FAMILY
Family worship
79. We assert our belief that the basic unit of the local church

is the family, and that the family at worship together is the idea for which we should strive. Children should be seen, within the Christian family, as fellow-children of God with their parents. We welcome the continuing growth of family worship as the liturgical threshold by which whole families are introduced to the life of the Church, and thus to Jesus Christ. Non-sacramental family services must not, however, become ends in themselves, but must lead on to participation in the full worship of the Church, including the sacraments.

Family evangelism and fellowship
80. Care must be taken lest this form of evangelism become child-orientated, and teaching consequently childish. The Church must labour in family-evangelism, as well as in child-evangelism, although we recognise the importance of the systematic instruction of children. Further, the distinction between adult and child, old and young, in the life of the Church, must not be too rigid. Christian fellowship, objectively expressed and fostered through liturgy, should break down barriers of age, and unite whole families more securely.

6. The Church and its Unity

Unity, truth and holiness
81. God's Church is one, as God is one. This oneness is God's gift to those who obey the gospel. It finds its proper expression when all the Christians of a locality appear as a single visible fellowship, united in truth and holiness, displayed in love, service and worship (especially at the Lord's Supper), and active in evangelism. The Church is to show its given oneness in order that the world may believe. Schisms, denominations, and exclusive forms of fellowship are contrary to the biblical ideal, yet in the past we have acquiesced in their existence. However, we cannot now rest content with a profession of being one in Christ with all believers if that profession becomes an excuse for refusing to seek local organic unity*. We

therefore not only reaffirm the general profession, but pledge ourselves to seek this specific goal. Yet this is not the only goal required of us. We must emphasise also the need to love and hold fast to the truth, to pursue holiness, and to practise evangelism. To join divided Christians in a way that would compromise these other ideals would be to miss God's will and to retard His work. So we dare not accept uncritically any and every proposed means to unity.

The local scene
82. We believe that under God means can be found which will promote unity, truth, holiness and evangelism simultaneously. Yet even these means will fail if they do not become the corporate concern of the local congregations involved. Too often wrong attitudes at the local level have meant that the cause of unity has been left to international congresses or inter-church commissions. We penitently seek God's grace to put away all such attitudes.

DIALOGUE
The need for conversations
83. A dialogue is a conversation in which each party is serious in his approach both to the subject and to the other person, and desires to listen and learn as well as to speak and instruct. The initial task for divided Christians is dialogue, at all levels and across all barriers. We desire to enter this ecumenical dialogue fully. We are no longer content to stand apart from those with whom we disagree. We recognise that all who 'confess the Lord Jesus Christ as God and Saviour according to the Scriptures and therefore seek to fulfil together their common calling to the glory of the one God, Father, Son and Holy Spirit' (World Council of Churches Basis) have a right to be treated as Christians, and it is on this basis that we wish to talk with them.

Learning together
84. This does not mean that we think all points of view

equally valid or all theological and ecclesiastical systems equally pleasing to God. It means only that we, who know ourselves to be prone to error and infected by sin, wish to join in conversation with others who are similarly affected, yet who profess to know God's grace, as we do. The aim is that together we may learn from the Bible what God by His Spirit has to say to us all.

Polemics at long range have at times in the past led us into negative and improverishing 'anti-'attitudes (anti-sacramental, anti-intellectual, *etc.*), from which we now desire to shake free. We recognise that in dialogue we may hope to learn truths held by others to which we have hitherto been blind, as well as to impart to others truths held by us and overlooked by them.

Mutual reformation

85. The Church is called to submit to Holy Scripture, and the Spirit is sent to interpret God's Word to His people. We do not suppose that Evangelicals have a monopoly of the Spirit's ministry in this regard. Through dialogue, therefore, we look to God to instruct and reform us all, and thereby to integrate us into one, through a deeper common grasp of His truth.

UNITY WITHIN THE CHURCH OF ENGLAND

Reform not separation

86. Dialogue and reformation should start at home. The chaos in doctrinal matters in the Church of England today causes us grief and shame. We reject the current tendency towards 'Christian agnosticism'* over the fundamentals of the gospel. In the face of this situation, however, it is reform that we desire, not separation. We look beyond Anglicanism as we now know it to a more biblical united Church.

Facing the future

87. We are deeply committed to the present and future of the Church of England. We believe that God has led us to this commitment, and we dare to hope and pray that through it God will bring His Word to bear with new power upon this

Church. We do not believe secession to be a live issue in our present situation. Only if the Church of England ceased to exhibit the marks of a true Church (see Article XIX of the 39 Articles) could such a step be contemplated.

Faith and order
88. We maintain that matters of faith take priority over matters of order. Our basic loyalty is to the Word of God and the people of God. While we accept that in England episcopacy seems the only pattern for reunion, we do not believe that it is a theological necessity. We affirm that regional Churches should be free to develop their own life, culture and forms of government.

INTERCOMMUNION*
Rival tables
89. The Lord's Supper is the focus of the Church's unity. Not only, therefore, is it wrong to exclude any of God's people from this feast; it is equally wrong that communion tables should exist in competition. Such a situation invites the local body of Christians to divide at a point where the duty to come together is strongest. Part of the goal of unity is the elimination of such situations.

The open table*
90. For good order the Church should appoint its officers to preside at the Supper, but there is no scriptural warrant for insisting that these must be bishops or episcopally ordained* presbyters. Therefore Anglicans should have freedom of conscience to communicate with the local church in any part of the world, be that church episcopal or non-episcopal. Where, as in England, the local church is divided into overlapping denominations, we stand firm on theological grounds in maintaining the traditional Anglican practice of an 'Open Table'.

Intercommunion
91. We welcome news that the provinces of Central, South

and West Africa have already approved the principle of inter-communion with non-episcopal Churches where a declared intention to unite exists, and that similar relations might be inaugurated at a future date between the Church of Scotland and Episcopal Church in Scotland. Where such an intention exists, the aim will be furthered by reciprocal intercommunion inasmuch as 'we who are many are one body, for we all partake of the same loaf' (1 Corinthians 10.17 RSV). We call on the Church of England to take similar action towards at least the Methodist Church, and also to enter into full communion with the Church of South India.

THE FREE CHURCHES
Reunion and reformation
92. The Free Churches* have close connections with us. We welcome their communicant members to Holy Communion, claiming biblical, moral and legal warrant for so doing. We acknowledge their ministries as true ministries of God's Church, and from time to time avail ourselves of them. We confess the guilt of the Church of England both in provoking dissent originally and in confirming and prolonging it by subsequent complacency and hostility. We desire reunion on the basis of mutual reformation, and we ask our Free Church brethren to join us in seeking this double blessing.

Our fellow Evangelicals
93. We value our present fellowship and co-operation with our fellow evangelicals in other Churches, to whom we are specially bound by a common understanding of the faith, and we desire a strengthening of these relations.

Obstacles to unity
94. Because we belong primarily to each other, we should not attach our loyalties unshakeably to denominations, buildings, organisations, particular ways of worship, or particular ministers. Such attachments betray immaturity in Christ. We recognise that when these loyalties become obstacles to *organic*

unity, they must be renounced, and we call upon all Anglican and Free Churchmen alike to recognise this too.

Jointly-owned buildings

95. In new areas of population, jointly-owned and jointly-used buildings are very necessary at the present time if the old divisions are not to become entrenched. Nevertheless, the rights of minority groups should not be overruled.

THE CHURCH OF ROME

96. We recognise that the Roman Catholic Church holds many fundamental Christian doctrines in common with ourselves. We rejoice also at signs of biblical reformation. While we could not contemplate any form of reunion with Rome as she is, we welcome the new possibilities of dialogue with her on the basis of Scripture, as exemplified in the recent appointment of a team of evangelical theologians to confer with Roman theologians.

THE ORTHODOX CHURCHES

97. We welcome the increasing opportunities of conferring with the Orthodox Churches, and we trust that Evangelicals will be fully represented in these conversations.

ANGLICAN-METHODIST REUNION

Full communion*

98. We look forward to the prospect of official full communion and eventual union with the Methodist Church, and call for intercommunion to be authorised as soon as a decisive commitment to unite has been made. We welcome every step towards the goal of union, and we call upon local congregations to prepare themselves for both the strains and the opportunities that such union will bring. We declare our concern that union should be with substantially the whole Methodist Church, and our resolve to oppose any scheme that will have the effect of needlessly dividing Methodism for the sake of union with us.

Unity commission

99. We deplore the restrictive terms of reference given to the Anglican-Methodist Unity Commission, especially in respect of the Service of Reconciliation. We regret the lack of dissentient Methodist representation.

Welcome improvements

100. We welcome the doctrinal statements of the March 1967 Interim Statement (*Towards Reconciliation*) as considerable improvements on those of 1963. We note with pleasure the statement on page 5 affirming the Commission's declared intention to 'preserve the present full communion which the Methodist Church enjoys with Methodist and other Churches lacking the historic episcopal succession throughout the Christian world' and its recognition of the 1964 Methodist Conference's understanding that 'these relations would at no stage be jeopardised'.

Service of Reconciliation

101. The Revised Service of Reconciliation contains many excellent features, but the mutual laying on of hands presents us with the same difficulties as it did in the 1963 Service. We recognise the difficulty which it is intended to solve (the probable unwillingness of most 'Catholic' churchmen to receive communion from Methodist ministers, which would close to Methodist ministers many doors of potential service among Anglicans, and delay the growth together of the two Churches). Nonetheless, we find the ceremony needless, misleading and a cause of offence. Despite all disclaimers, it has the effect of calling in question the status of Methodist ministers which to us is beyond question. If the service incorporating the ceremony is made to precede the official inauguration of intercommunion, it will also have the effect of making the sacrament of Holy Communion appear as a function of a certain sort of ministry; though if intercommunion should precede the Service of Reconciliation, this difficulty would be eased.

While we suspend decision till the final report, at this

stage few of the clergy among us would feel able to commit themselves to take part in the Service of Reconciliation.

We welcome the guarantee (*Towards Reconciliation*, page 4) that non-attendance at the Service of Reconciliation will not affect a minister's status in his own Church.

South India – The Solution?

102. We call upon the Convocations, in conjunction with the Methodist Conference, even at this late stage, to instruct the Anglican-Methodist Unity Commission to consider 'the South India Method'* as an alternative to the present scheme, so that the Churches may then choose between the two. We believe that, despite the problems and strains involved, this gives the greatest promise of spiritual health and further reunion.

Glossary to the Statement

The words listed are mostly technical terms which are sometimes used in different ways by different people. The defini-
tions given indicate the sense in which the terms are to be
understood in the *Statement*.

Benefice
A benefice is a freehold (*q.v.*) office, held by a clergyman who
is called the incumbent or minister. According to the nature
of his benefice he is also styled rector or vicar or perpetual
curate. He has the right to the proceeds of the benefice until
his death or until it is legally vacated by him.

Charismatic
Formed from *charisma* (*grace-gift*, Greek), this word expresses
the claim that movements or manifestations to which it is
applied spring from gifts of the Holy Spirit.

Child-centred education
Child-centred education puts the main emphasis upon the
experience of the child, and relates the subject being taught
to what the child is and knows.

Content-centred education
Content-centred, (or 'subject-centred') education puts the emphasis on the facts to be taught, instead of asking whether the
child's experience has any relation to those facts.

'Christian agnosticism'

Querying the truth or the possibility of knowing the truth of Christian redemptive facts while professedly retaining Christian trust in God.

Episcopal ordination
The bestowal of ministerial commission with laying-on of hands and prayer by a bishop standing in the historic succession.

Establishment
The word in an ecclesiastical context is used to mean the Church 'as by law established' in any country, as the public or state-recognised form of religion, with certain privileges, and certain obligations. Establishment can take many different forms, but the process of establishment means that the state has accepted that particular Church – (in England, the Church of England) as the proper religious body to have an official position as the teacher of the faith and the provider of pastoral care for the nation. The state gives to such a Church a certain legal position, and certain legal sanctions to its decrees, and also claims for itself a measure of control in church affairs.

Free Churches
The term has come to be applied to the major Protestant Churches in England who 'dissent from' or are 'free from' the Church of England as by law established (*q.v.*). These would include the Presbyterians (in England, though not of course in Scotland), the Congregationalists, Methodists, Baptists, Society of Friends, and Christian Brethren. Its use is often extended to a wide variety of smaller Churches, including various Pentecostal Churches, and to bodies such as the Salvation Army.

Freehold
'To have the freehold' is a convenient way of saying that an incumbent or minister is in possession of a freehold benefice (*q.v.*) from which he can be removed only on certain

comparatively well-defined grounds. Apart from these he has the right to the proceeds of the benefice until his death, or until it is legally vacated by him. It is this security of tenure that is one of the distinguishing marks of the freehold office or benefice enjoyed by vicars and rectors at present, as against the position of a priest-in-charge or an assistant curate, or the appointment for a term of years only which the *Pastoral Measure* (now before the Church Assembly) proposes for *e.g.* the newly-styled 'vicars' of a team ministry (*q.v.*), and in some cases the 'rector' also.

Full Communion
Unrestricted sacramental fellowship between churches of different denominations, 'including the mutual recognition of ministries' (*Lambeth Conference* 1958, 2.24).

Group Ministry
A term at present often employed loosely to mean simply a number of parishes or clergymen working in co-operation, but used in this Statement in the sense described below.

As defined by the *Pastoral Measure* (at present before the Church Assembly) the words 'Group Ministry' will take on the distinctive meaning of a group of benefices (*q.v.*) in which the following provisions apply.

First, each of the incumbents in the group shall have authority to minister in each of the benefices in the group (though under the directions of the particular incumbent concerned). *Second*, it shall be the duty of the incumbents in the group to meet regularly together to discuss their work, and to assist each other in making the best pastoral provision for the group as a whole.

No incumbent may be appointed to any benefice within the group without the bishop's approval, following consultation with other incumbents in the group; and no incumbent may resign from his membership without resigning his benefice.

Intercommunion
Recognised reciprocal interchange of communicants between churches of different denominations.

'Open Table', The
'Open Table' means open communion. Welcoming to the Lord's Table communicants from other denominations, irrespective of whether a reciprocal welcome is extended or not.

Organic Unity
Organic unity is organic union. Enjoyment by local churches in full communion with each other of a common life sufficiently integrated at organisational level to show that they are one body and family in Christ, and only one.

Patronage
As commonly used in church affairs, the word means the right to present a person of the patron's choice to an ecclesiastical benefice (*q.v.*). It includes presentation to bishoprics and the like, but more commonly to parochial responsibility. Every parish has a patron, who may be for example, the Crown, the bishops, a dean and chapter, the incumbent of a mother church, a Diocesan Board of Patronage, a College, a private individual, or a Patronage Trust or Society.

It is the patron's duty, when a parish loses its incumbent, to act under the provisions of the *Benefice (Exercise of Rights and Presentation) Measure 1931* and consult with the parochial church council with a view to nominating the new incumbent to the bishop.

Important provisions also appear in legislation on, for example, pastoral reorganisation or in connection with benefice property, requiring that the patron must be consulted.

Rebaptism
Baptism, on the basis of professed faith and repentance, of a person who has been baptised before, normally in infancy. To Baptists generally, the baptising as adults of those baptised in

infancy is not rebaptism, but baptism, since, in their view this must be preceded by a personal profession of faith.

'Situation ethics'
The view that nothing is prescribed to the Christian, as of absolute and perpetual obligation, save love to his neighbour, and that the specific moral laws of Scripture are rules of thumb to which love may rightly make exceptions when the situation is felt so to require.

'South India method', The
(As adopted at the inauguration of the Church of South India in 1947.) Entry by episcopal and non-episcopal Churches into full communion (*q.v.*) and organic union (*q.v.*) under an episcopal form, without an initial laying-on of hands by a bishop upon ministers lacking episcopal ordination (*q.v.*).

Synodical Government
A system of Church government, set out in the Report *Government by Synod* (Church Information Office, 1966) by means of a General Synod or Council, formed by reconstituting the present Church Assembly. There would also be provision for diocesan synods, and for ruridecanal synods. The aim of synodical government, in whatever form, would be to secure 'that the ultimate authority and right of collective action lie with the whole body, the Church'.[1]

Team Ministry
A term at present often employed loosely to mean simply a number of clergymen working in co-operation, but used in this statement in the sense described below.

   As defined by the *Pastoral Measure* (at present before the Church Assembly) the words 'Team Ministry' will take on the distinctive meaning of the sharing of the cure of souls

---

[1]See page 14 of *Government by Synod* for this quotation from the 1958 Report *The Convocations and the Laity*.

in a particular area by a team of ministers under the following provisions. The leader of the team will have the title of *rector*, and may have the freehold (*q.v.*). The others shall be called *vicars*, and shall be appointed only for a term of years. The rector shall have general responsibility for the pastoral work of the area, though vicars may also have special responsibilities (either for an area, or for a particular pastoral function) which may be independent of the rector's general oversight. Rector and vicars shall meet regularly together to discuss the work of the team.

Succeeding rectors shall be appointed either by a patronage board set up when the Team Ministry is begun (and in this case the bishop *must* be chairman) or by the Diocesan Board of Patronage, or by the bishop if he is already sole patron of the benefice (*q.v.*). Vicars in the team shall be chosen by the bishop and the rector jointly, after consultation with the parochial or district church council.

The Keele Statement is used by kind permission of the Church Pastoral Aid Society, Warwick, England. It was first published by CPAS in 1967.

Appendix B: A Basis of Faith for the Anglican Evangelical Assembly

1. *Introduction*

   As members of the Church of England within the one, holy, catholic, and apostolic Church we *affirm* the faith uniquely revealed in the holy Scriptures and set forth in the catholic creeds, of which faith the Thirty Nine Articles of Religion are a general exposition. Standing in the Reformation tradition we lay especial emphasis on the grace of God – his unmerited mercy – as expressed in the doctrines which follow.

2. *God as the Source of Grace*

   In continuity with the teaching of holy Scripture and the Christian creeds, *we worship* one God in three Persons – Father, Son and Holy Spirit. God has created all things, and us in his own image; all life, truth, holiness, and beauty come from him. His Son Jesus Christ, fully God and fully man, was conceived through the Holy Spirit and born of the Virgin Mary, was crucified, died, rose and ascended to reign in glory.

3. *The Bible as the Revelation of Grace*

   We receive the canonical books of the Old and New Testaments as the wholly reliable revelation and record of God's grace, given by the Holy Spirit as the true word of God written. The Bible has been given to lead us to salvation, to be the ultimate rule for Christian faith and conduct, and the supreme authority by which the Church must ever reform itself and judge its traditions.

4. *The Atonement as the Work of Grace*

   We believe that Jesus Christ came to save lost sinners. Though sinless, he bore our sins, and their judgment, on the cross, thus accomplishing our salvation. By raising Christ bodily from the dead, God vindicated him as Lord and Saviour and proclaimed his victory. Salvation is in Christ alone.

5. *The Church as the Community of Grace*
   We hold that the Church is God's covenant community, whose members, drawn from every nation, having been justified by grace through faith, inherit the promises made to Abraham and fulfilled in Christ. As a fellowship of the Spirit manifesting his fruit and exercising his gifts, it is called to worship God, grow in grace, and bear witness to him and his Kingdom. God's Church is one body and must ever strive to discover and experience that unity in truth and love which it has in Christ, especially through its confession of the apostolic faith and in its observance of the dominical Sacraments.

6. *The Sacraments as the Signs of Grace*
   We maintain that the Sacraments of Baptism and Holy Communion proclaim the gospel as effective and visible signs of our justification and sanctification, and as true means of God's grace to those who repent and believe. Baptism is the sign of forgiveness of sin, the gift of the Spirit, new birth to righteousness and entry into the fellowship of the People of God. Holy Communion is the sign of the living, nourishing presence of Christ through his Spirit to his people; the memorial of his one, perfect, completed and all-sufficient sacrifice for sin, from whose achievement all may benefit but in whose offering none can share; and an expression of our corporate life of sacrifical thanksgiving and service.

7. *Ministry as the Stewardship of Grace*
   We share, as the people of God, in a royal priesthood common to the whole Church, and in the community of the Suffering Servant. Our mission is the proclamation of the gospel by the preaching of the word, as well as by caring for the needy, challenging evil and promoting justice and a more responsible use of the world's resources. It is the

particular vocation of bishops and presbyters, together with deacons, to build up the body of Christ in truth and love, as pastors, teachers, and servants of the servants of God.

8. *Christ's Return as the Triumph of Grace*
   We look forward expectantly to the final manifestation of Christ's grace and glory when he comes again to raise the dead, judge the world, vindicate his chosen and bring his Kingdom to its eternal fulfilment in the new heaven and the new earth.